List of Contents

Introduction

In the realm of investing, where fortunes are won and lost in the blink of an eye, the name Warren Buffett shines as a beacon of timeless wisdom and enduring success. His journey from a humble paper route to the pinnacle of wealth and influence is the stuff of legend, a tale we will delve into shortly.

This book is not a mere collection of financial strategies and stock-picking techniques. It is a pilgrimage into the heart and mind of one of the most enigmatic figures in the history of finance. It is an exploration of the principles and philosophies that have not only shaped Warren Buffett's remarkable success but have also withstood the test of time, offering a beacon of hope to every individual who aspires to build lasting wealth through prudent investing.

As we delve into the chapters that follow, we will traverse the landscapes of value investing, dissect the intricacies of option strategies, and uncover the art of constructing a resilient portfolio. Yet, before we embark on this intellectual odyssey, it is imperative that we pause to reflect on the essence of Warren Buffett's legacy.

Warren Buffett's life is a testament to the enduring power of knowledge, patience, and unwavering commitment to one's principles. It is a story of a young boy from Omaha, Nebraska, who, armed with an insatiable curiosity, embarked on a lifelong quest for wisdom. It is a narrative of a man who transformed himself from a humble newspaper delivery boy into one of the wealthiest individuals on the planet, all the while staying true to his core values and beliefs.

Buffett's journey is not defined by overnight successes or get-rich-quick schemes. Instead, it is marked by the slow and steady accumulation of wealth, the patient cultivation of a circle of competence, and the disciplined adherence to a set of principles that have become the bedrock of his investment philosophy. It is a journey that stands in stark contrast to the frenetic pace of modern markets, where speculators often chase short-term gains at the expense of long-term stability.

In the chapters that follow, we will explore the intricacies of value investing, a philosophy that underpins Buffett's approach to the market. We will delve into the concept of intrinsic value, the notion of economic moats, and the importance of a margin of safety. These are not mere theoretical constructs but practical tools that have guided Buffett in his investment decisions for decades.

We will also peer into the world of options, a realm where Buffett has ventured with characteristic prudence. Here, we will demystify the intricacies of options trading and understand how Buffett has harnessed their potential to enhance returns and manage risk. While options may appear complex to the uninitiated, we will unravel their simplicity and explore how they can be integrated into an investment strategy that aligns with the principles of value investing.

As we navigate these investment landscapes, we will not only gain insights into Buffett's strategies but also glean valuable lessons on risk management, portfolio construction, and the importance of a long-term perspective. We will uncover the art of patience, a virtue that has allowed Buffett to weather market storms and emerge stronger on the other side.

But this journey is not solely about financial acumen; it is also a journey of self-discovery. It is an invitation to reflect on our own financial goals, risk tolerance, and investment philosophies. It is an opportunity to align our actions with our aspirations and forge a path toward financial success that is both prudent and sustainable.

As we embark on this expedition into the world of Warren Buffett's investing wisdom, let us carry with us the spirit of curiosity, the commitment to learning, and the resolve to embrace the enduring principles that have illuminated his path. For it is not just about winning in the investing game; it is about winning with integrity, wisdom, and a steadfast commitment to the principles that endure beyond the vagaries of the market.

Chapter 1: The Wisdom of Warren Buffett

1.1: A Brief Biography of Warren Buffett

In the modern history of investing, there stands a figure whose wisdom has transcended the bounds of Wall Street to touch the lives of ordinary individuals seeking financial success. Warren Buffett, a name synonymous with shrewdness and sagacity in the realm of finance, has etched his legacy in the annals of investing history. To embark upon a journey to win like Buffett, we must first delve into the captivating story of his life.

Buffett's Early Years and Influence

Warren Edward Buffett, widely regarded as one of the greatest investors of all time, was born on August 30, 1930, in Omaha, Nebraska. His early years played a pivotal role in shaping the man who would later become an investment icon. From the outset, Buffett displayed an exceptional aptitude for numbers and an insatiable curiosity about the world of finance.

Growing up in Omaha, Buffett was surrounded by a family that encouraged his intellectual growth. His father, Howard Buffett, was a stockbroker and a Congressman, which provided young Warren with a unique perspective on the world of finance and politics. It was within this nurturing environment that Buffett's interest in investing was first ignited.

As a young boy, Buffett displayed his entrepreneurial spirit by engaging in various money-making ventures. His first foray into business was delivering newspapers, and he quickly grasped the significance of saving and investing. By the age of 11, he had purchased his first shares of stock, showing an early penchant for investing that would set the stage for his future success.

Buffett's Investment Journey

Warren Buffett's investment journey truly began when he entered the hallowed halls of Columbia Business School, where he studied under the legendary Benjamin Graham, a pioneer of value investing. Graham's teachings would leave an indelible mark on Buffett's investment philosophy. Under Graham's mentorship, Buffett absorbed the principles of value investing like a sponge, learning to focus on the intrinsic value of a company rather than its short-term market fluctuations.

Upon completing his education, Buffett embarked on his professional career. He worked briefly as a securities analyst and later as a partner at an investment firm, all while steadily honing his investment acumen. In 1956, he founded Buffett Partnership Ltd., an investment partnership that would serve as the breeding ground for his early success.

One of the most defining moments of Buffett's investment journey came in 1965 when he acquired a textile company called Berkshire Hathaway. Though the textile business itself eventually proved to be a poor investment, Buffett used the company as a vehicle to deploy his value investing strategy. He transformed Berkshire Hathaway into a diversified conglomerate, redirecting its cash flows into more promising investments. Over time, it became the cornerstone of his investment empire.

The Buffett Philosophy

At the heart of Warren Buffett's investment philosophy lies a profound simplicity and discipline that sets him apart. His adherence to timeless principles has not only delivered remarkable financial success but has also provided a roadmap for countless investors seeking to replicate his achievements.

One of the central tenets of the Buffett philosophy is his emphasis on long-term thinking. Buffett has always maintained that his favorite holding period for a stock is "forever." This unwavering commitment to the long term aligns with his belief that the stock market should be viewed as a place to buy and hold ownership in quality companies, rather than a venue for speculative trading.

Moreover, Buffett's philosophy extols the virtues of patience and discipline. He advises investors to remain unflinchingly patient in their investment decisions, avoiding impulsive reactions to market fluctuations. This approach is underpinned by his famous saying: "The stock market is designed to transfer money from the Active to the Patient."

Buffett's investment style also emphasizes the concept of a "margin of safety." He advocates purchasing stocks when they are trading below their intrinsic value, providing a buffer against market downturns. This margin of safety, he argues, not only protects investors from losses but also enhances the potential for long-term gains.

Warren Buffett's journey from a curious young boy in Omaha to a revered investment guru is a testament to the enduring principles that underlie his success. His early exposure to finance, tutelage under Benjamin Graham, and unwavering commitment to simplicity, patience, and value investing have cemented his status as a paragon of the investing world.

1.2 The Power of Value Investing

Warren Buffett, often referred to as the "Oracle of Omaha," has achieved legendary status in the world of investing. His remarkable success can be attributed, in large part, to his unwavering commitment to a specific investment philosophy: value investing. In this sub-chapter, we will embark on a journey to understand the profound principles that underpin value investing, exploring what it means to identify intrinsic value and the concept of economic moats.

Understanding Value Investing

At the core of Warren Buffett's investment philosophy lies the bedrock principle of value investing. This approach is grounded in the belief that financial markets are not always rational and can often misprice assets, creating opportunities for astute investors. Value investors, like Buffett, seek to capitalize on these mispricings by identifying stocks that are undervalued relative to their intrinsic worth.

Value investing begins with the fundamental belief that in the long run, the stock market tends to align with the intrinsic value of the underlying assets. In other words, over time, the market tends to reward companies whose stock prices are below their true worth and penalize those whose prices are unjustifiably high.

This principle is rooted in the notion that the market can be irrational in the short term but becomes rational over extended periods. As value investors, we capitalize on these temporary market inefficiencies, understanding that they offer opportunities for significant profit when corrected.

Value investing transcends mere stock picking; it's a mindset, a disciplined approach to investing that demands patience, a critical eye, and a long-term perspective. To truly comprehend value investing, one must grasp the following key points:

* Contrarian Thinking: Value investors do not follow the crowd. They are contrarians, willing to swim against the tide when market sentiment veers into irrational exuberance or unwarranted fear. Warren Buffett himself has emphasized that "be fearful when others are greedy, and be greedy when others are fearful." This contrarian mindset is a cornerstone of value investing.

* Intrinsic Value: At the heart of value investing is the concept of intrinsic value. In simple terms, intrinsic value is what a stock is truly worth, irrespective of its market price. It is the present value of a company's future cash flows, taking into account factors such as growth prospects, competitive advantage, and risk. Identifying intrinsic value requires a deep understanding of the company's fundamentals and the ability to differentiate between price and value.

* Margin of Safety: Value investors are risk-averse by nature. They insist on a "margin of safety" when making investment decisions. This means buying a stock at a price significantly below its calculated intrinsic value, providing a cushion against potential downside risks. Buffett often likens this concept to buying a dollar bill for 50 cents, ensuring that even if your valuation is slightly off, you still stand to gain.

Identifying Intrinsic Value

Identifying intrinsic value is the crux of value investing. It's a meticulous process that involves a comprehensive analysis of a company's financials, industry dynamics, and competitive position. Here's a closer look at the key elements of this critical step:

* Financial Analysis: Scrutinizing a company's financial statements, including its balance sheet, income statement, and cash flow statement, is fundamental to determining intrinsic value. This analysis helps assess the company's financial health, profitability, and growth potential. Key

financial ratios, such as price-to-earnings (P/E) and price-to-book (P/B), are valuable tools in this evaluation.

* Qualitative Assessment: Intrinsic value is not solely about numbers; it also encompasses qualitative factors. Understanding the company's management team, its corporate culture, and its competitive advantage in the industry is essential. Buffett places great importance on investing in companies with durable competitive moats, which we will explore shortly.

* Discounted Cash Flow (DCF) Analysis: One of the most widely used methods for estimating intrinsic value is the discounted cash flow (DCF) analysis. This involves projecting a company's future cash flows and discounting them back to their present value. The DCF method accounts for the time value of money, providing a comprehensive valuation framework.

Economic Moats and Competitive Advantage
Warren Buffett often likens a successful investment to buying a castle with an impenetrable moat around it. The concept of an economic moat refers to a company's sustainable competitive advantage—a unique position that allows it to fend off competition and maintain profitability over the long term. Understanding economic moats is pivotal in value investing:

* Types of Moats: There are various forms of economic moats, including brand loyalty, network effects, cost advantages, and regulatory advantages. Companies

possessing these moats are less susceptible to competitive threats and can command pricing power.

* Investing in Moat-Builders: Buffett's investment philosophy heavily favors businesses that are adept at building and widening their moats over time. These companies consistently reinvest in their core operations, innovate, and adapt to changing market conditions. By investing in moat-builders, value investors align their portfolios with companies poised for enduring success.

* Long-Term Orientation: Economic moats thrive when investors take a long-term view. Buffett himself is renowned for his commitment to holding investments for extended periods, allowing the power of compounding and the strengthening of moats to work in his favor.

In essence, the power of value investing lies not in speculation or market timing but in a disciplined, research-driven approach that seeks to uncover businesses with intrinsic value and economic moats. It is a method that values substance over style, patience over impulsiveness, and rationality over emotions.

1.3 Why You Should Invest like Buffett

Warren Buffett, often referred to as the Oracle of Omaha, stands as a towering figure in the world of investing. His track record of consistent success over several decades has garnered him a following of devout investors and made him a household name. What sets Buffett apart and why should you consider following in his footsteps?

Buffett's Consistent Success

Warren Buffett's consistent success in the world of investing is nothing short of legendary. For decades, he has outperformed the broader market and delivered remarkable returns for his shareholders at Berkshire Hathaway. But what exactly accounts for this remarkable track record?

At the heart of Buffett's success lies a steadfast commitment to the principles of value investing. He possesses a keen ability to identify undervalued assets and companies with strong competitive advantages. Instead of chasing short-term gains or speculating on market trends, Buffett's approach is grounded in the timeless concept of intrinsic value.

Intrinsic value, in Buffett's eyes, represents the true worth of an asset or business. This value is determined by a careful analysis of a company's financials, earnings potential, and its ability to withstand economic downturns. Buffett's discipline in calculating intrinsic value allows him to identify opportunities when the market undervalues a business. It's a patient and deliberate approach that stands in stark contrast to the frenetic trading that often characterizes Wall Street.

Common investors can learn a valuable lesson from this aspect of Buffett's strategy. Rather than being swayed by market noise or daily price fluctuations, they can embrace a long-term perspective, rooted in a deep understanding of the assets they hold. By focusing on intrinsic value and patiently waiting for the market to recognize it, investors can build a solid foundation for their portfolios.

The Long-Term Approach

Warren Buffett is renowned for his unwavering commitment to long-term investing. He famously quipped that his preferred holding period for a stock is "forever." While the idea of holding an investment indefinitely may seem radical in a world of fast-paced trading, it embodies the essence of Buffett's approach.

This long-term perspective is rooted in several key beliefs. First and foremost is the recognition that the stock market is inherently volatile and unpredictable in the short term. Prices can swing wildly based on a myriad of factors, from economic data to geopolitical events. Buffett understands that trying to time these short-term movements is a fool's errand.

Instead, he advocates for a patient and disciplined approach that values the power of compounding. Over time, investments can grow exponentially, delivering substantial returns to those who are willing to hold through market ups and downs. This perspective not only reduces the stress of constantly monitoring market movements but also allows investors to benefit from the gradual appreciation of their assets.

Buffett's long-term approach also emphasizes the importance of holding quality investments. By thoroughly researching and selecting businesses with strong fundamentals and competitive advantages, he minimizes the need for constant portfolio adjustments. This strategy aligns perfectly with common investors who may lack the time and resources for frequent trading.

How Buffett's Strategies Benefit Common Investors
Perhaps the most compelling reason for common investors to embrace Warren Buffett's strategies is their accessibility and adaptability. Unlike complex financial instruments or esoteric trading techniques, Buffett's approach is straightforward and can be applied by investors of all levels of experience.

One of the key tenets of Buffett's strategy is that it doesn't require a vast amount of capital to begin. Whether you have a modest sum or a substantial portfolio, the principles of value investing and long-term thinking can be tailored to your specific circumstances. This inclusivity makes Buffett's approach truly democratic and applicable to the common investor.

Furthermore, Buffett's strategies are characterized by their transparency. He openly shares his investment philosophy through annual shareholder letters and interviews, making his wisdom readily available to anyone interested in learning. This level of transparency contrasts with the opacity often associated with Wall Street, where complex financial products and hidden fees can leave investors in the dark.

Additionally, Buffett's approach is time-tested and proven. The principles of value investing and a long-term perspective have consistently delivered results, even in the face of economic downturns and market crises. For common investors seeking a reliable and robust approach to building wealth over time, Buffett's strategies provide a solid foundation.

Warren Buffett's consistent success, long-term perspective, and the accessibility of his strategies make a compelling case for common investors to adopt his approach. By understanding the principles of value investing, embracing a patient outlook, and leveraging the power of compounding, individuals can navigate the world of investing with confidence and aim to achieve their financial goals over the long haul.

Part I: Mastering Value Investing

Chapter 2: Intrinsic Value Analysis

2.1 Calculating Intrinsic Value

The ability to determine the true worth of an asset is the bedrock of value investing, a philosophy that has guided the likes of Warren Buffett through decades of successful investing. In this sub-chapter, we embark on a journey to demystify the intricate process of calculating intrinsic value, using three fundamental approaches: Discounted Cash Flow (DCF) Analysis, Comparables Analysis, and the insightful utilization of Historical Data.

Discounted Cash Flow (DCF) Analysis

At the heart of value investing lies the belief that the future cash flows generated by an investment should be the primary driver of its present value. The Discounted Cash Flow (DCF) analysis is the compass that helps us navigate through this financial terrain.

Imagine, for a moment, that you are holding a crystal ball that allows you to peek into the future financial performance of a company. This crystal ball, in essence, is what DCF analysis strives to achieve - albeit in a more methodical and mathematical manner.

This technique takes a bird's-eye view of a company's expected cash flows—both positive and negative—over the course of its existence. The crux lies in predicting these cash flows accurately. This requires a profound understanding of the company's historical financial performance, market dynamics, and a crystal-clear vision of its future prospects.

The DCF calculation involves discounting these future cash flows back to their present value using an appropriate discount rate. Herein lies the beauty and complexity of the DCF analysis—determining the correct discount rate, often referred to as the "required rate of return." Buffett has emphasized the importance of using a discount rate that reflects the risk associated with the investment. For many, this rate is derived from the cost of capital, considering both debt and equity components.

But why is the DCF analysis so crucial, and how does it align with Buffett's strategy? The answer lies in his emphasis on the intrinsic value of a business. By meticulously forecasting future cash flows and discounting them back to their present value, the investor arrives at an estimate of what the business is truly worth.

To calculate the intrinsic value of an investment using DCF, we follow a simple yet profound equation:

$$IV = \frac{CF}{(1+r)^t}$$

Where:

* IV stands for Intrinsic Value
* CF represents the expected Cash Flow
* r denotes the discount rate, often associated with the rate of return an investor requires
* t signifies the time period at which the cash flow is expected

At first glance, this equation may seem formidable, but the underlying concept is surprisingly intuitive. It essentially tells us that the value of future cash flows diminishes over time, with the rate of diminishment dictated by the discount rate. The higher the discount rate, the more the future cash flows are discounted, reflecting a greater level of risk or opportunity cost.

Consider a practical example. Suppose we are evaluating a company, and our analysis indicates that it is expected to generate $1,000,000 in cash flow annually for the next 10 years. If our required rate of return, or discount rate, is 10%, the intrinsic value of the company can be calculated as follows:

$$IV = \frac{1,000,000}{(1+0.10)^1} + \frac{1,000,000}{(1+0.10)^2} + \cdots + \frac{1,000,000}{(1+0.10)^{10}}$$

Now, you might be thinking that manually calculating this for 10 years seems daunting. Thankfully, financial tools and software make the computation effortless. What's critical is understanding the principle - that cash received in the future is worth less to us today due to the opportunity cost of not having that money available for investment elsewhere.

However, it's important to remember that forecasting the future is an inherently uncertain endeavor, and Buffett himself acknowledges this challenge. He advises that investors should err on the side of caution, being conservative in their estimates rather than overly optimistic. In essence, the DCF analysis is a rigorous exercise that demands patience and diligence, aligning perfectly with Buffett's long-term, value-driven approach.

Comparables Analysis

While DCF analysis is a robust method for calculating intrinsic value, it's not the sole approach in the investor's toolkit. Comparables Analysis, also known as the Market Approach, offers an alternative perspective. This approach leans on the notion that similar assets should have similar valuations.

To illustrate this concept, picture yourself in a bustling real estate market. When determining the value of a house, you might look at recent sales prices of similar houses in the neighborhood. If houses with similar square footage, amenities, and location have sold for $500,000, it's reasonable to assume that your house, which shares those characteristics, is also worth around $500,000.

In the world of investing, Comparables Analysis operates in much the same way. Investors identify comparable companies or assets, analyze their market valuations, and use that information to estimate the intrinsic value of the asset they are interested in.

Buffett's approach to comparables analysis is grounded in his belief in the importance of a margin of safety. He recommends that investors focus on companies that are not just attractively valued but also have a strong competitive position and sustainable moats. In essence, while comparables analysis provides a valuable benchmark, Buffett's wisdom reminds us that it should be used in conjunction with a deeper understanding of the business and its competitive advantages.

Using Historical Data

History has an uncanny way of repeating itself, and when it comes to investing, historical data is a treasure trove of insights. In our quest to determine intrinsic value, delving into the annals of historical performance can be illuminating.

One of the key lessons from Buffett's approach to using historical data is the importance of consistency and predictability. He gravitates toward companies with a track record of stable and growing earnings, viewing them as less risky and more likely to weather economic downturns.

Consider a company that has consistently demonstrated growth in its earnings per share (EPS) over the past decade. This historical trend suggests that the company possesses a competitive advantage or a resilient business model. By examining the historical financial statements, we can identify patterns and trends that can inform our intrinsic value calculation.

Furthermore, historical data allows us to assess a company's ability to weather economic downturns. Did the company maintain profitability during the last recession? How did it fare compared to its peers? These questions, answered through historical analysis, can help us gauge the company's resilience and potential to generate future cash flows.

Calculating intrinsic value is a cornerstone of value investing. The DCF analysis provides a rigorous method for estimating value based on expected future cash flows. Comparables Analysis offers a perspective grounded in market valuations, while the prudent use of historical data adds a layer of context and insight. As we continue our journey through the world of investing, remember that mastering these techniques is akin to wielding a powerful compass that can guide you toward sound investment decisions. It's a skill that has served Warren Buffett and many successful investors well, and it's a skill that you, too, can develop and refine over time.

2.2 Economic Moats and Competitive Advantage

In the realm of investing, particularly in the style of Warren Buffett, the concept of an "economic moat" holds a place of paramount importance. The term itself invokes imagery of a protective barrier that shields a castle from intruders. In the world of business and investment, an economic moat is, metaphorically, that protective fortress around a company's profits, preventing competitors from storming the gates and laying siege to its market share.

Identifying such moats is a crucial skill in value investing, one that Warren Buffett has honed to perfection over the years. When you look at a company, you're not merely assessing its current financial health or stock price; you're attempting to gauge the sustainability of its competitive advantages.

Identifying Moats

Economic moats, as envisioned by Buffett, act as protective barriers around a company's business. They are like formidable castles that shield a company from the onslaught of competition. To be a truly discerning investor, one must be adept at identifying these moats and appreciating their significance.

At the heart of economic moats lies the idea that certain businesses possess unique attributes that make it difficult for competitors to encroach upon their territory. These attributes can manifest in various forms, and it's imperative for investors to recognize them.

One of the most common forms of an economic moat is a brand. Consider the Coca-Cola Company, an investment long favored by Buffett. The Coca-Cola brand is a paragon of the enduring power of a strong, recognized label. It's a brand that has strong presence into of our culture, transcending generations and geographical boundaries. This brand recognition provides Coca-Cola with a pricing power that few can rival.

Another manifestation of an economic moat is what we call a network effect. Think of social media platforms like Facebook or payment processors like Visa. The more people use these services, the more valuable they become. This creates a self-reinforcing cycle where the network grows stronger with each new user. Competitors find it exceedingly challenging to breach the walls of such entrenched networks.

Cost advantages can also be a form of an economic moat. Consider a company like Amazon. Its vast distribution network, coupled with its efficient operations, allows it to offer lower prices than many competitors. This cost advantage makes it formidable and keeps competitors at bay.

Sustainable Competitive Advantages
Identifying an economic moat is one thing; ensuring that it remains sustainable is another. Not all moats are created equal, and their durability is a critical factor in an investor's assessment. A sustainable competitive advantage is one that can withstand the test of time, remaining relevant and potent for years, if not decades.

One way to gauge the sustainability of a competitive advantage is to examine the factors that underpin it. For instance, a patent may provide a temporary advantage, but what happens when it expires? On the other hand, a deeply ingrained brand or a vast network is more likely to endure.

Consider the case of Coca-Cola once again. Its brand, while not impervious to change, has remained an influential force in the beverage industry for over a century. It continues to be a symbol of refreshment and enjoyment, demonstrating the staying power of a strong brand.

The ability to adapt and innovate is another hallmark of a sustainable competitive advantage. Companies that can pivot in response to changing market conditions are better equipped to withstand challenges. Think of how Apple transitioned from a computer company to a leader in smartphones and wearables. Its commitment to innovation and adaptation has been instrumental in maintaining its competitive edge.

Examples from Buffett's Portfolio

Warren Buffett's investment portfolio serves as an instructive guide when it comes to understanding the practical application of economic moats and sustainable competitive advantages. His investments in companies like Coca-Cola, Apple, and American Express provide valuable case studies.

Coca-Cola's enduring brand and global distribution network have been a cornerstone of Buffett's investment philosophy. He recognized the company's ability to generate consistent cash flows and its dominant position in the beverage industry. These attributes, rooted in economic moats, made it an attractive long-term investment for Buffett.

Buffett's investment in Apple, one of the world's leading technology companies, reflects his appreciation for sustainable competitive advantages. Apple's ecosystem, with its integrated hardware, software, and services, creates a seamless and compelling user experience. This ecosystem has fostered customer loyalty and retention, serving as a robust competitive advantage.

American Express, another stalwart in Buffett's portfolio, exemplifies the power of a trusted brand and customer loyalty. The company's premium credit card offerings and focus on affluent customers have contributed to its resilience and profitability. Its economic moat, built on a reputation for reliability and service, has stood the test of time.

Buffett's investments are not merely a collection of stocks; they are a masterclass in the identification and exploitation of economic moats and sustainable competitive advantages. His success as an investor underscores the enduring value of these concepts in the world of investing.

The pursuit of economic moats and sustainable competitive advantages is a quest for timeless investment wisdom. Identifying these moats, appreciating their sustainability, and drawing inspiration from Buffett's investments can empower investors to navigate the complex landscape of stocks with confidence and clarity. These concepts form the bedrock of intelligent, long-term investing and offer a pathway to winning like Buffett in the world of investing.

2.3 Margin of Safety

"Margin of Safety", the key of treasure. In the world of investing, this principle stands as a bedrock of wisdom, a guiding light that has illuminated the path for the likes of Warren Buffett and countless other successful investors. In this sub-chapter, we'll embark on a journey to comprehend the essence of the Margin of Safety, its profound relevance, and how we can seamlessly integrate it into our investing endeavors.

Defining Margin of Safety

At its core, the Margin of Safety is a concept that encapsulates prudence and rationality in investing. It is the protective buffer, the financial cushion that investors build beneath their investments. To define it succinctly, the Margin of Safety represents the difference between the intrinsic value of an asset or investment and its market price.

Intrinsically, it's akin to buying a dollar for less than a dollar, a simple yet profound idea. The concept stems from the realization that no matter how well we analyze and scrutinize an investment, there remains an inherent degree of uncertainty in the markets. Prices can fluctuate due to various factors, often irrational and unpredictable, and they can depart from the true worth of an asset.

Imagine you are considering purchasing a house. Its intrinsic value, based on a meticulous assessment of its location, condition, and potential rental income, stands at $200,000. However, the market price, influenced by current trends, emotional buyer sentiment, or even macroeconomic factors, is $180,000. The Margin of Safety in this scenario is $20,000, the gap between what you believe the house is worth and what you're paying for it.

Why It Matters

Now, why is this Margin of Safety so imperative in the world of investing? To answer this, we must recognize the inherent unpredictability of markets and the inherent risks that accompany investing.

Markets are prone to swings of irrational exuberance and pessimism. Fear and greed can steer prices far from their intrinsic values. It's during these turbulent times that the Margin of Safety becomes your steadfast companion, offering protection from the whims of the crowd.

Consider a scenario where you purchase a stock for $50 per share, and after a period of market turbulence, its price plummets to $30 per share. If your diligent analysis reveals the intrinsic value of the stock to be $40 per share, you have a Margin of Safety of $10 per share. This safety net mitigates potential losses and provides the confidence to stay the course, rather than succumbing to panic.

Moreover, the Margin of Safety is an antidote to investment mistakes. Even the most astute investors occasionally make errors in judgment. By adhering to the principle of buying assets with a Margin of Safety, one can absorb the impact of such mistakes without enduring catastrophic losses. It grants the freedom to learn from errors without suffering irrevocable financial consequences.

Applying Margin of Safety in Investing

The practical application of the margin of safety is where its true value emerges. It demands a disciplined approach to investing, one that requires patience, rigorous analysis, and a willingness to wait for the opportune moment.

For example of a stock with an intrinsic value of $100 and a market price of $80. To fully harness the margin of safety, an investor might consider purchasing the stock only when it is trading at a significant discount to its intrinsic value. In doing so, they build a robust defense against market volatility.

Moreover, the margin of safety compels investors to approach financial analysis with utmost diligence. It necessitates a thorough examination of a company's financials, industry dynamics, and competitive advantages. By leaving no stone unturned, investors can better assess the inherent risks and opportunities within an investment.

Warren Buffett's adherence to the margin of safety principle is well-documented. He famously quipped, "The stock market is designed to transfer money from the Active to the Patient." His approach embodies the essence of the margin of safety, emphasizing the significance of buying quality assets at discounted prices and allowing time to work its magic.

Now that we've grasped the essence and significance of the Margin of Safety, let's explore how we can incorporate it into our investment strategy.

1. Valuation Discipline: Begin by meticulously assessing the intrinsic value of an asset or investment. This involves a rigorous analysis of financial statements, competitive advantages, growth prospects, and potential risks. A thorough understanding of the business or asset is paramount.

2. Determining the Buy Price: Once you've calculated the intrinsic value, establish a clear buy price—the price at which you are willing to acquire the asset. This buy price should provide a comfortable Margin of Safety, typically a percentage below the calculated intrinsic value.

3. Patience and Discipline: Be patient and disciplined in your approach. It's not uncommon for markets to offer opportunities with an ample Margin of Safety during periods of volatility or pessimism. Resist the temptation to chase after popular assets at inflated prices.

4. Portfolio Diversification: Utilize the Margin of Safety principle to construct a diversified portfolio of assets. By spreading your investments across various asset classes, industries, and geographies, you further mitigate risks and enhance the stability of your portfolio.

5. Regular Reevaluation: Markets evolve, and economic conditions fluctuate. It's imperative to regularly reassess the Margin of Safety in your investments. As prices fluctuate,

your Margin of Safety may increase or decrease, necessitating adjustments to your portfolio.

The Margin of Safety serves as your shield against the unknown in the world of investing. It empowers you to make rational, level-headed decisions in the face of market turbulence and uncertainty. It's a principle that not only aligns with the wisdom of Warren Buffett but also stands as a timeless beacon for every prudent investor, reminding us that success in investing often hinges on not just what we buy but, crucially, what we pay for it.

Chapter 3: Stock Selection

3.1 Quality vs. Price

In the world of investing, there is a perpetual tug-of-war between quality and price. Warren Buffett, the legendary investor we've been learning from throughout this book, is often hailed as a champion of value investing. But what exactly does value investing entail, and why does it place such a strong emphasis on quality and price?

Balancing Quality and Price

Warren Buffett once aptly remarked, "It's far better to buy a wonderful company at a fair price than a fair company at a wonderful price." This dictum encapsulates the essence of stock selection - the delicate equilibrium between quality and price.

Quality in the context of stocks pertains to the underlying company's fundamentals. It encompasses factors such as a durable competitive advantage, robust financials, competent management, and a history of sustainable growth. Quality equates to a company's ability to endure and thrive over time, even in the face of economic headwinds.

Price, on the other hand, is the market's valuation of the stock at any given moment. It represents the consensus of investors' perceptions and expectations. The price you pay for a stock determines your potential return on investment. Pay too much, and your margin of safety diminishes; pay too little, and you risk missing out on substantial gains.

Buffett's genius lies in his knack for finding high-quality companies trading at prices lower than their intrinsic value. This is where the artistry of balancing quality and price comes into play. When selecting stocks, ask yourself: "Am I getting a high-quality company at a reasonable price?"

Achieving this balance entails rigorous research and a deep understanding of the businesses you're investing in. Start by identifying companies with strong economic moats – a concept we explored in an earlier chapter – as they are more likely to maintain their quality over time.

Additionally, assess a company's financial statements to gauge its fiscal health. Look for consistent revenue and earnings growth, a manageable debt load, and a history of generating positive free cash flow. A company with a solid financial foundation is better equipped to weather economic downturns.

Furthermore, scrutinize the management team. Competent, shareholder-oriented leadership is an invaluable asset. A management team with a long-term vision and a track record of prudent capital allocation is more likely to enhance shareholder value.

But how do you determine the price at which a stock becomes attractive? This leads us to the next key point.

Avoiding Overvalued Stocks

In a market driven by euphoria and sentiment, it's all too easy to get swept up in the fervor of rising stock prices. However, seasoned investors, like Warren Buffett, emphasize the importance of avoiding overvalued stocks. Paying too much for a stock can erode your potential returns and expose you to unnecessary risks.

Overvaluation occurs when a stock's market price far exceeds its intrinsic value. It's akin to buying a dollar bill for two dollars – a proposition that no rational investor should entertain. Overvalued stocks are often associated with exuberant market sentiment and lofty expectations, which can be unsustainable in the long run.

To identify overvalued stocks, employ various valuation metrics. Common methods include price-to-earnings (P/E) ratio, price-to-sales (P/S) ratio, and price-to-book (P/B) ratio. Compare these metrics to historical averages and industry peers to gauge whether a stock is trading at an inflated valuation.

Remember, overvaluation doesn't necessarily mean a stock is a poor investment; it simply means that you may be paying a premium for future growth prospects. Assess the risks and potential rewards carefully, and be prepared to exercise discipline by passing on overvalued opportunities.

Identifying Undervalued Gems
While avoiding overvalued stocks is crucial, the real allure of stock selection lies in identifying undervalued gems – those hidden treasures that have yet to be fully recognized by the market. This is where the astute investor's acumen shines, and it's an area in which Warren Buffett has consistently excelled.

To uncover undervalued gems, start by employing valuation metrics, as mentioned earlier. However, focus on stocks that not only appear undervalued but also possess the hallmarks of quality we discussed earlier. Seek out companies with strong competitive advantages, resilient business models, and sound financials.

Additionally, pay attention to market sentiment and short-term fluctuations. Mr. Market, as Buffett affectionately refers to the collective mood of the market, can be prone to irrational exuberance or pessimism. Use these market swings to your advantage. When pessimism reigns and stocks are unduly punished, it may present an opportune moment to acquire shares of high-quality companies at a discount.

Warren Buffett's stock selection prowess is underpinned by his unwavering commitment to long-term investing. He views stocks not as mere pieces of paper that fluctuate in price but as fractional ownership stakes in actual businesses. By meticulously balancing quality and price, avoiding overvalued stocks, and identifying undervalued gems, you can follow in Buffett's footsteps and enhance your odds of success in the complex world of stock selection.

3.2 Buffett's Investment Checklist

In the world of investing, Warren Buffett's name is synonymous with success. His consistent ability to select stocks that deliver superior returns over the long term is nothing short of legendary. But what exactly goes on in Warren Buffett's mind when he's selecting stocks? What is the checklist that guides him through this complex and high-stakes process? In this sub-chapter, we will delve deep into Buffett's investment checklist and explore the criteria he employs for stock selection. By the end of this journey, you'll gain insights into how to identify promising investment opportunities and make rational decisions, avoiding the pitfalls of impulsive choices.

Buffett's Criteria for Stock Selection

The foundation of Warren Buffett's stock selection process lies in a set of well-defined criteria. These criteria serve as a filter, allowing only the most promising stocks to make their way into his portfolio. Let's examine these criteria one by one.

1. Sustainable Competitive Advantage: At the heart of Buffett's criteria is the concept of a sustainable competitive advantage, often referred to as an economic moat. Buffett looks for companies that have built strong barriers around their businesses, protecting them from competitors. These barriers can take various forms, such as brand recognition, patents, scale, and network effects. When a company possesses a durable competitive advantage, it can maintain its profitability and market position over the long haul.

2. Predictable and Understandable Businesses: Buffett has a preference for businesses with straightforward and understandable models. He tends to shy away from complex and highly speculative industries. This preference stems from his belief that understanding the business is paramount to making rational investment decisions. By investing in businesses he can readily grasp, Buffett reduces the likelihood of making costly mistakes due to ignorance or misinformation.

3. Earnings Consistency: Another essential criterion for Buffett is the consistency of a company's earnings. He seeks businesses with a track record of stable and predictable earnings over time. This consistency is a testament to the company's ability to weather economic downturns and continue generating profits, even in challenging environments. It provides a level of comfort to investors, knowing that their investment is in a financially sound company.

4. A Long-Term Perspective: Buffett's investment horizon is measured not in days or months but in years and decades. He seeks companies with the potential for sustained growth and value creation over the long term. This long-term perspective aligns with his value investing philosophy, which emphasizes holding investments for extended periods, allowing the power of compounding to work its magic.

The Importance of Understanding the Business
A critical aspect of Buffett's stock selection process is his deep understanding of the businesses he invests in. He believes that investing in a company without a clear comprehension of its operations is akin to gambling. Therefore, he takes the time to study a company's business model, industry dynamics, competitive landscape, and management team.

Understanding the business goes beyond merely reading financial statements. It involves gaining insights into how the company generates revenue, its cost structure, and the factors that could impact its future growth. Buffett's emphasis on understanding the business allows him to make informed decisions and assess whether a company's competitive advantage is sustainable. This is 3 thing you should stick when understanding the business;

The Circle of Competence: Buffett famously advises investors to stay within their circle of competence – an area where they have a deep understanding. He practices what he preaches, and this principle is a cornerstone of his investment philosophy. He invests in businesses that he can comprehend fully. Understanding a business means grasping not just its products or services but also its industry dynamics, competitive landscape, and growth prospects. Buffett's stock selections are often rooted in industries and businesses he understands well.

The Dangers of Speculation: Buffett distinguishes between investing and speculation. He shies away from businesses and industries he finds too complex or unpredictable. He cautions against investing in companies with obscure or convoluted business models. By sticking to what he understands, Buffett avoids the pitfalls of speculative investing and reduces the risk of making impulsive decisions based on market hype or short-term trends.

The Power of Momentum: Understanding a business also requires patience. Buffett's approach is rooted in the belief that, over time, the market recognizes the true value of a fundamentally strong company. He emphasizes the importance of having the discipline to hold onto investments through market fluctuations. This long-term perspective allows him to weather market volatility and benefit from compounding returns. It's a lesson in the virtue of patience and the power of time in the world of investing.

Moreover, this understanding helps him see through short-term market fluctuations and noise. It enables him to stay focused on the long-term potential of a business, even when others may be swayed by short-term volatility or market sentiment.

Avoiding Impulsive Decisions

One of the most remarkable qualities of Warren Buffett's investment approach is his discipline in avoiding impulsive decisions. He understands the emotional rollercoaster that investing can be, and he has mastered the art of staying calm and rational during market turbulence.

Buffett's commitment to avoiding impulsive decisions is rooted in his adherence to his investment criteria and principles. When the market is in turmoil, he doesn't let fear or greed dictate his actions. Instead, he relies on his checklist and the fundamental analysis he has conducted on a company. If a stock meets his criteria and offers an attractive margin of safety, he may use market volatility as an opportunity to buy more shares, rather than succumbing to panic selling.

By adhering to his checklist and maintaining discipline, Buffett has been able to capitalize on market downturns, accumulating positions in high-quality companies at discounted prices.

Warren Buffett's investment checklist serves as a powerful tool for stock selection. It incorporates criteria that emphasize the importance of sustainable competitive advantage, understanding the business, consistency, and a long-term perspective. Additionally, it highlights the significance of avoiding impulsive decisions in the face of market fluctuations. By adopting these principles and incorporating them into your own investment approach, you can enhance your ability to identify promising investment opportunities and navigate the complex world of stock selection with confidence.

3.3 The Art of Patience

Stock selection is a critical aspect of any investor's journey, and it's an area where Warren Buffett has truly excelled over the years. In this sub-chapter, we'll delve into one of the most remarkable aspects of Buffett's approach—his patience. We'll explore how he approaches the waiting game, the immense power of long-term thinking, and his method for navigating the inevitable ups and downs of the market.

Buffett's Approach to Waiting

Patience is a virtue often touted in the world of investing, and nobody personifies this better than Warren Buffett. His approach to waiting is not just about being patient for the sake of it; it's about having a clear strategy behind the waiting game.

One of the cornerstones of Buffett's approach to waiting is his belief in thorough research and understanding of the businesses he invests in. He doesn't rush into decisions; instead, he takes the time to study a company's financials, competitive advantages, and management team. This careful consideration helps him build conviction in his investments.

Buffett's waiting game is also deeply rooted in his belief in the principle of "buy and hold." He doesn't buy stocks with the intention of selling them in the near future. Instead, he holds them for the long term, often for decades. This patient approach allows his investments to compound over time, generating substantial wealth.

Moreover, Buffett doesn't get swayed by short-term market fluctuations or the noise of daily trading. He remains focused on the underlying fundamentals of the companies he's invested in. This steadfastness is a key reason for his success.

The Power of Long-Term Thinking

Buffett's incredible success can be attributed, in large part, to his unwavering commitment to long-term thinking. He doesn't concern himself with the daily or even yearly market gyrations. Instead, he takes a multi-decade view when it comes to his investments.

Long-term thinking provides several advantages. First and foremost, it aligns with the power of compounding. Buffett understands that over time, investments can grow exponentially if left untouched. This allows him to capitalize on the full potential of his investments.

Furthermore, taking a long-term perspective frees an investor from the emotional rollercoaster of short-term market movements. Market volatility and sudden price swings become less intimidating when viewed in the context of a decades-long investment horizon.

Long-term thinking also encourages patience and discipline. It discourages impulsive decision-making and the temptation to chase after the latest hot stock. Instead, it promotes a steady, rational approach to investing.

Navigating Market Volatility

While the stock market offers the potential for substantial returns over the long term, it's not without its share of turbulence. Market volatility, characterized by sharp price fluctuations and periodic downturns, is an inherent part of investing. Buffett's approach to navigating this volatility is a masterclass in itself.

One of Buffett's famous quotes encapsulates his outlook on market volatility: "Be fearful when others are greedy and greedy when others are fearful." This timeless wisdom underscores his willingness to see market downturns as opportunities rather than threats.

During market turbulence, Buffett often seizes the chance to buy great companies at discounted prices. For Buffett, market volatility presents buying opportunities rather than reasons to sell. He often quips that the stock market is the only place where things go on sale, and people run out of the store. During market downturns, he deploys his patient approach to add to his positions in quality companies at attractive prices. His patience and financial discipline allow him to remain calm and rational when others are panicking. This contrarian approach has consistently paid off in the long run.

Buffett's ability to navigate market volatility is also informed by his historical perspective. He studies past market cycles and crises to gain insights into how markets behave during times of stress. This knowledge helps him avoid knee-jerk reactions and make informed decisions based on the lessons of history.

The art of patience, as practiced by Warren Buffett, is not just about sitting idle. It's a deliberate, strategic approach to investing that involves careful research, a long-term perspective, and the ability to navigate market volatility with a steady hand. By understanding and adopting these principles, common investors can emulate Buffett's success and build wealth over the long term. Remember, in the world of investing, patience truly is a virtue.

Part II: Utilizing Options in Your Portfolio

Chapter 4: Options Demystified

4.1 Understanding Options Basics

In the vast world of investing, where strategies can be as diverse as the individuals employing them, options stand out as a formidable tool. Not different with Warren Buffet approach, the options is one of his main arsenal. Yet, for many, options remain enshrouded in mystery, their potential obscured by a lack of understanding. In this sub-chapter, we embark on a journey to unravel this mystique, stripping away the complexity to reveal the fundamental essence of options trading.

What Are Options?

Options, in the world of finance, are contracts that grant the holder the right but not the obligation to buy (call option) or sell (put option) an underlying asset at a specified price (strike price) on or before a predetermined date (expiration date). Let's dissect this definition.

Imagine you're eyeing a valuable piece of real estate, a beautiful old house. You'd love to have it, but you're not entirely sure whether it's the right time to buy. So, you enter into an agreement with the homeowner that allows you to decide whether you want to purchase the house at a fixed price within the next six months. This agreement is your "call option" on the house. It provides you the choice but not the obligation to buy it.

Now, think of the opposite scenario. You already own that vintage house, and you're concerned that its value might decrease in the future. To protect yourself, you enter into an agreement with someone that gives them the right (but not the obligation) to buy the house from you at a specific price within the next six months. This is your "put option" on the house. It provides you with a safeguard against potential price declines.

Options are like the keys to a financial puzzle. They give you the flexibility to adapt your investment strategy as the market unfolds. With options, you can hedge against potential losses, generate income, and even speculate on price movements.

Types of Options
Options come in two main flavors: call options and put options. Let's take a closer look at each.

1. Call Options: A call option provides the holder with the right, but not the obligation, to buy an underlying asset at a specified price (strike price) before or on the expiration date. Call options are often used by investors who anticipate that the price of the underlying asset will rise. By purchasing a call option, you gain the ability to buy the asset at a predetermined, lower price, allowing you to profit from the price difference.

Think of it as reserving a table at your favorite restaurant. You don't have to commit to dining there, but you have the option to do so at a set price.

2. Put Options: On the flip side, a put option grants the holder the right, but not the obligation, to sell an underlying

asset at a specified price (strike price) before or on the expiration date. Put options are often used as insurance against potential price declines in an asset. By holding a put option, you have the ability to sell the asset at a guaranteed, higher price, even if the market value drops.

It's akin to taking out an insurance policy on your car. You hope you won't need it, but it provides peace of mind knowing that you're protected if an accident occurs.

Other than two distinction above, options can be categorized based on several factors, including the duration of the contract, the underlying asset, and the exercise style.

Duration: Options come in various maturities, ranging from short-term to long-term. European options can only be exercised at expiration, while American options can be exercised at any time before or on the expiration date.

Underlying Asset: While stocks are the most common underlying assets, options can be based on a wide array of assets, including commodities, currencies, and indices. These are known as equity options, commodity options, currency options, and index options, respectively.

Exercise Style: Options can also differ in terms of their exercise style. In addition to European and American options, there are Asian options, Bermudan options, and more, each with unique exercise characteristics.

Options Terminology

Before we dive deeper into the world of options, let's familiarize ourselves with some essential terminology that will be instrumental in our journey:

1. Strike Price: Also known as the exercise price, this is the price at which the holder of the option has the right to buy (for call options) or sell (for put options) the underlying asset. The strike price plays a pivotal role in determining the profitability of an option.

2. Expiration Date: Every option has a predetermined date on which it expires. After this date, the option ceases to exist, and the holder loses the right to exercise it. Time is a critical factor in the world of options, as it affects their value.

3. Premium: The premium is the price paid by the option buyer to the option seller (also known as the writer) for the rights conveyed by the option. It's the cost of obtaining the option and is influenced by factors such as the underlying asset's price, volatility, and time remaining until expiration.

4. In-the-Money (ITM), At-the-Money (ATM), and Out-of-the-Money (OTM): These terms describe the relationship between the strike price and the current market price of the underlying asset. An option is said to be in-the-money if it has intrinsic value (profit potential if exercised immediately), at-the-money if the strike price equals the current market price, and out-of-the-money if it has no intrinsic value.

Imagine you have a call option to buy a share of a company at $50, and the current market price of that share is $55. Your call option is in-the-money because you could exercise it and make an immediate profit of $5 per share.

Now that we've peeled back the layers of options, it's clear that they offer a world of opportunities and strategies to investors. Whether you're looking to safeguard your investments, generate income, or speculate on price movements, options can be a powerful tool in your financial toolkit.

4.2 The Role of Options in Buffett's Strategy

Warren Buffett's investment strategy is often synonymous with value investing and long-term wealth accumulation. However, what sets him apart from many other investors is his judicious use of options, a versatile financial instrument that he has skillfully incorporated into his investing toolkit. In this sub-chapter, we'll explore the intricate role of options in Warren Buffett's investment strategy, focusing on how he employs them, enhances returns, and effectively manages risk.

How Buffett Uses Options

Warren Buffett's approach to options is rooted in prudence and strategic thinking. He employs them as a means to further optimize his investment portfolio. Here we can see how to use of options can be encapsulated in three primary strategies:

1. Income Generation: One of favorite uses of options is generating income. Investor often sells covered call options on stocks he already owns in his portfolio. By selling call options, we earns premiums, effectively receiving a payment from the buyer of the option. In return, we obligates to sell our stock at a specified strike price if the buyer chooses to exercise the option. This strategy allows us to monetize our existing holdings while potentially profiting from the appreciation of the stock, all while maintaining ownership.

For example of this strategy, In Apr 1993, Buffett sold 50,000 put options (equivalent of 5 million shares) for $1.50 worth of premiums per option in Coca Cola stock. Coca Cola shares were trading at $39 back in Apr 1993. This comes up to a total of $7.5 million in premiums collected. These options expire on 17 Dec 1993 with an exercise price of $35.

Other than that, Buffet's frequently uses index options to generate income. One of notable use Warren show is selling index put options to generate premium. About this strategy will discuss later in next chapter.

2. Insurance against Market Volatility: Investors not immune to market turbulence. To safeguard our portfolio from the occasional market downturns,we purchases put options, offering us the right (but not the obligation) to sell a stock at a predetermined price within a specified period.

These put options act as insurance, ensuring that we can limit potential losses if the market takes a significant dip.

3. Acquisition Financing: When Investor seeks to acquire a company, we can often utilizes options as part of our financing strategy. Investor may negotiate an agreement with the target company that provides us with options to purchase shares at a favorable price in the future. This approach allows us to secure a potential acquisition while mitigating risk, as we only exercises the options if the investment proves profitable.

Enhancing Returns with Options
Warren Buffett's adept use of options is not limited to risk management; it also plays a pivotal role in enhancing returns on his investments. Here's how options come into play:

1. Leveraging Capital Efficiently: Buffett's investment philosophy is to put capital to work effectively. Options can amplify our capital efficiency by allowing us to control larger positions with less upfront capital. For instance, instead of buying a large quantity of a stock, we might opt for call options, giving us the right to purchase the stock at a set price. This approach magnifies our potential returns if the stock appreciates.

2. Monetizing Holdings without Selling: As mentioned earlier, Investors can sells covered call options on stocks we owns. This allows us to generate additional income without selling the underlying assets. By collecting

premiums from call options, we enhances the overall return on our investment portfolio.

3. Timing Market Entries: Options can be used to time market entries strategically. When Investors identifies an attractive investment but believes that market conditions may improve in the short term, we might use options to gain exposure to the asset while deferring the actual purchase. This approach enables us to benefit from potentially better entry points.

Risk Management with Options
Risk management is at the heart of Warren Buffett's investment strategy, and options play a vital role in this aspect. Here's how options contribute to investors risk management framework:

1. Downside Protection: As mentioned earlier, We can uses put options to protect our portfolio from significant market declines. These options act as a safeguard, allowing us to sell assets at predetermined prices, thereby limiting potential losses. This downside protection aligns with our focus on preserving capital.

2. Margin of Safety: Buffett's emphasis on a margin of safety is reflected in his use of options. By employing options judiciously, he builds an additional layer of safety into his investments. This risk mitigation strategy ensures that even if the market behaves unpredictably, he has predefined exit strategies in place.

3. Risk Diversification: Through the strategic use of options, We effectively diversifies risk in our portfolio. Rather than relying solely on traditional asset allocation, we hedges our positions with options, reducing the potential impact of adverse market movements on our overall portfolio.

Options are not merely a peripheral component of Warren Buffett's investment strategy; they are a cornerstone of his approach to preserving and enhancing wealth. Buffett's adept use of options, whether for generating income, enhancing returns, or managing risk, exemplifies his pragmatic and disciplined approach to investing. As common investors seek to emulate his success, understanding and incorporating these options strategies into their own portfolios can be a valuable step toward winning like Warren Buffett in the investing game.

4.3 The Risks and Rewards of Options

In the intricate realm of investing, options often stand as both an alluring prospect and a perplexing puzzle. In this sub-chapter, we'll unravel the multifaceted nature of options trading, delving deep into the potential rewards, the accompanying risks and downsides, and the paramount task of finding that elusive equilibrium.

Potential Rewards

In the world of investing, options present a unique opportunity. They offer the possibility of significant rewards that can far exceed those available through traditional equity investments. However, with this potential for reward comes a corresponding level of risk. It is crucial for investors to understand these rewards before diving into the world of options.

First and foremost, options provide a leveraged position in the underlying asset. This means that with a relatively small investment, an options trader can control a much larger position in the underlying asset. For instance, purchasing a call option on a stock allows you to benefit from the stock's price appreciation without actually owning the shares. This leverage can amplify your gains when the market moves in your favor.

Options also offer flexibility. There are various strategies that can be employed to tailor your risk-reward profile to your specific goals and market outlook. For example, writing covered calls can generate income from existing stock holdings while limiting potential gains. Alternatively, buying long-term call options can provide exposure to significant upside potential with a defined and limited risk.

Another advantage of options is their versatility in different market conditions. Whether the market is bullish, bearish, or range-bound, there are option strategies that can be used to capitalize on the prevailing sentiment. This adaptability is one of the reasons why options have become an integral part of professional traders' toolkits.

However, it's important to remember that while options can offer substantial rewards, they are not without their risks.

Risks and Downsides

Options can be a double-edged sword. While they offer the potential for substantial rewards, they also come with a range of risks that investors must carefully consider.

One of the primary risks associated with options is the risk of losing the entire investment. Unlike stocks, where the downside is limited to the purchase price, options can expire worthless, resulting in a 100% loss of the premium paid. This risk is particularly pertinent for buyers of options, as they have a finite lifespan. Therefore, it's crucial to select options with expiration dates that align with your investment horizon. For seller, you practically have unlimited loss risk since you forced to cover the option trade if buyer of options decide to exercise their options.

Another risk is the complexity of options strategies. Options involve various components, including strike prices, expiration dates, and different combinations of calls and puts. This complexity can lead to confusion and costly mistakes for inexperienced investors. It's essential to thoroughly understand the mechanics of each strategy and their potential outcomes before implementing them.

Moreover, options trading can be highly speculative, and it's easy to fall into the trap of overtrading. The allure of quick profits can lead some investors to take excessive risks, such as buying out-of-the-money options with the hope of a significant price move. Such strategies can result in rapid losses if the market doesn't behave as anticipated.

Market volatility is another risk factor in options trading. Elevated volatility can lead to wider bid-ask spreads and increased option premiums, making it more expensive to establish positions. Additionally, sudden and unexpected market events can cause rapid price swings, impacting options values and potentially resulting in unexpected losses.

Lastly, options require constant monitoring and adjustment, especially for strategies that involve multiple positions. Failing to manage options positions actively can lead to unexpected outcomes and increased risk exposure.

Finding the Right Balance
Navigating the world of options requires finding the delicate balance between risk and reward. To do so effectively, investors should approach options with a well-defined strategy and a clear understanding of their objectives.

One key principle is to never risk more than you can afford to lose. Given the potential for significant losses in options trading, it's essential to allocate only a portion of your investment capital to options. Diversifying across various assets, including stocks, bonds, and cash, can help mitigate the risks associated with options.

Additionally, education and practice are crucial. Before trading options with real capital, consider using paper trading or virtual platforms to gain experience and refine your strategies. Understanding the intricacies of options, including how they respond to changes in volatility and time decay, is essential for making informed decisions.

Moreover, risk management tools, such as stop-loss orders and position sizing, can help limit potential losses. Implementing these tools as part of your options trading strategy can provide a safety net and protect your capital.

Successful options traders also maintain a long-term perspective. While options offer the allure of quick profits, it's essential to view them as part of a broader investment strategy. Avoid making impulsive decisions based on short-term market fluctuations and focus on your overall financial goals.

Options can be a powerful tool for investors, offering the potential for substantial rewards and portfolio diversification. However, they are not without their risks. To make the most of options trading, it's imperative to understand both the rewards and risks, employ prudent risk management strategies, and maintain a disciplined and long-term approach. By finding the right balance between risk and reward, investors can harness the full potential of options in their investment journey.

Chapter 5: Index Options: A Key to Success

5.1 Introduction to Index Options

In the ever-evolving world of investing, where strategies abound and financial instruments proliferate, index options have emerged as a compelling and versatile tool for investors seeking to navigate the complexities of the market. As we delve into this sub-chapter, we embark on a journey to demystify index options, shedding light on their nature, advantages, and the pivotal role they play in shaping a resilient investment portfolio.

What Are Index Options?

At its core, an index option represents a financial contract that grants its holder the right, but not the obligation, to buy or sell an underlying stock index at a predetermined price within a specified time frame. To grasp this concept fully, let's break it down.

Firstly, we have the term 'index.' An index, in the context of investing, is a meticulously constructed benchmark that measures the performance of a specific group of stocks. These indices are designed to mirror the overall performance of the stock market or a particular sector, offering investors a snapshot of how a predefined basket of equities is faring.

Now, let's move to the 'option' part. An option, be it a call option or a put option, grants the holder the right to make a choice. In the case of index options, it's the choice to buy (call option) or sell (put option) the underlying index at a predetermined price, known as the strike price, on or before a specified expiration date.

Consider an illustrative example: You hold a call option on the S&P 500 index with a strike price of 4,000 and an expiration date of three months from now. This option gives you the right to purchase the S&P 500 index at 4,000, regardless of its current market price, within the next three months. If the index's value exceeds 4,000 during this period, you can exercise your option and buy it at the agreed-upon price, potentially profiting from the price difference.

Conversely, a put option on the same index would allow you to sell the index at the strike price of 4,000, providing a valuable hedge against potential market downturns.

Benefits of Index Options

The allure of index options lies in their unique set of benefits, each serving a distinct purpose in the investor's toolkit.

1. Portfolio Diversification: Index options offer exposure to entire markets or sectors, allowing investors to diversify their portfolios without the need to buy individual stocks. This diversification can mitigate risk and enhance long-term stability.

2. Risk Management: In the ever-volatile world of finance, risk management is paramount. Index options provide a means to hedge against market downturns, serving as insurance for your portfolio. A well-placed put option can

act as a shield when turbulence strikes, preserving capital and buying time for rational decision-making.

3. Leverage with Limited Risk: One of the remarkable attributes of options, including index options, is their ability to provide leverage. With a comparatively modest upfront investment, an investor can gain exposure to a more substantial underlying asset. However, unlike trading stocks on margin, the potential losses with options are limited to the initial investment—a crucial feature for prudent investors.

4. Versatility in Strategy: Index options are versatile tools that can be employed in various strategies. From straightforward calls and puts to complex strategies like covered calls, iron condors, and straddles, these instruments offer a rich palette for crafting tailored investment strategies.

5. Capital Efficiency: Index options offer an efficient way to allocate capital. By using options to gain exposure to an index, investors can free up capital for other investments or maintain a more diversified portfolio with the same capital base.

The Role of Index Options in a Portfolio
Now that we have a firm understanding of what index options are and the benefits they bring, let's explore their role in constructing a well-rounded investment portfolio.

In essence, index options can serve as a valuable complement to a broader investment strategy. They can help investors achieve specific goals, such as generating income, protecting capital, or enhancing returns, all while maintaining exposure to the broader market.

Imagine a scenario where you hold a diversified portfolio of individual stocks but are concerned about an impending market correction. Here's where index put options come into play. By purchasing put options on a relevant index, you can protect your entire portfolio against a market downturn, acting as a safeguard for your hard-earned gains.

On the other hand, if you seek to generate additional income from your portfolio, writing covered call options on an index you hold in your portfolio can provide a consistent stream of premiums, potentially enhancing your overall returns.

Furthermore, for investors with a bullish outlook, index call options can amplify your gains when the market moves in your favor, capitalizing on upward trends with leverage.

In sum, index options, when used judiciously, can be an integral part of your investment strategy, offering a dynamic range of possibilities to safeguard, enhance, and diversify your portfolio.

While index options hold significant potential, they also come with risks and complexities that require careful consideration. So, you must carefully calculated your risk before taking more steps.

5.2 Buffett's Approach to Index Options

Warren Buffett, the Oracle of Omaha, is renowned for his steadfast commitment to value investing. Yet, even within this unwavering philosophy, he has made strategic forays into the world of index options. Contrary to what one might expect from a value investing icon, Buffett's thoughtful approach to these financial instruments reveals an underlying principle: adaptability.

How Buffett Utilizes Index Options

Buffett's employment of index options is no haphazard maneuver; it's a calculated strategy that aligns with his investment philosophy. So, how exactly does he make use of index options to his advantage?

1. Generating Additional Income: One of the primary purposes of index options in Buffett's portfolio is income generation. He often writes (sells) put options on broad-market indices, such as the S&P 500. When an investor purchases a put option, they are essentially paying for insurance against a market decline. By selling these options, Buffett collects premiums, essentially getting paid for providing this insurance.

Consider this scenario: Buffett sells put options with a strike price below the current market level. If the market remains stable or rises, he keeps the premium as profit. If the market drops significantly, and the options are exercised, he buys the underlying assets (usually high-quality stocks) at a lower price, effectively getting them at a discount. This dual-purpose strategy allows him to generate income in bull markets and acquire assets at favorable prices during market downturns.

2. Hedging Existing Positions: While Warren Buffett is an advocate of long-term investing, he doesn't shy away from employing index options for hedging purposes. In times of market uncertainty or when he anticipates potential short-term turbulence, he may use put options to protect his existing portfolio. This aligns with his principle of preserving capital and avoiding permanent loss.

For instance, if he holds a substantial amount of stocks in his portfolio and foresees a possible market correction, he might buy put options as insurance. These options will increase in value as the market falls, offsetting losses in his stock holdings. This pragmatic approach allows him to safeguard his capital without the need to sell off his long-term investments prematurely.

The Advantages of Index Options
Buffett's strategic use of index options provides several advantages that align with his investment philosophy and long-term orientation.

1. Risk Mitigation: One of the most significant benefits of index options is risk mitigation. By selling put options and collecting premiums, Buffett is effectively reducing the risks associated with his investments. Even in a bear market, the premiums received from options can cushion the impact of declining stock prices, providing a degree of downside protection.

2. Income Generation: Index options offer a source of income that can complement the dividends from his stock holdings. This additional income can be reinvested or used to finance new investments, further compounding his wealth over time. Buffett's approach to options reflects his penchant for making money work for him, even in the short term.

3. Leverage with Prudence: Buffett's use of index options allows him to leverage his investments prudently. By selling put options, he can control a more substantial amount of assets than he would with just the cash on hand. This leverage amplifies his returns when markets are rising, but it's managed cautiously to minimize risks.

Real-Life Examples from Buffett's Investments
Buffett's application of index options is not a mere theoretical construct; it's a strategy he has employed effectively in his own investments. A notable example is his well-documented use of index put options in the lead-up to the financial crisis of 2008.

In the years preceding the crisis, Buffett recognized the frothiness of financial markets and the looming housing bubble. As a precautionary measure, he entered into a significant position in index put options on various indices, including the S&P 500. When the crisis struck and stock markets plummeted, these options provided a substantial buffer, mitigating the impact of the downturn on Berkshire Hathaway's portfolio.

During the 2008 financial crisis, Buffett seized the opportunity to utilize index options effectively.

Recognizing the heightened market volatility and the potential for further declines, he wrote (sold) long-term put options on several major stock indices. This move not only generated substantial premiums but also positioned him to benefit if the market rebounded, as it eventually did.

Additionally, Buffett's use of index call options as an income-generating strategy is evident in his investment in the insurance industry. Berkshire Hathaway's ownership of insurance companies, such as GEICO, generates significant premiums. These premiums, in essence, serve as a form of option income, where policyholders pay premiums in exchange for insurance coverage.

Buffett's approach to index options exemplifies his versatility as an investor. He doesn't confine himself to one-dimensional strategies but rather leverages a wide array of financial instruments to achieve his objectives while staying true to his core principles of value investing and risk management.

Warren Buffett's approach to index options reflects his wisdom in navigating the complexities of financial markets. By utilizing these instruments for risk mitigation and income generation, he exemplifies the versatility and adaptability that have made him a legendary figure in the world of investing. Index options, when wielded with prudence and a long-term perspective, can indeed be a key to success in the investing game, as demonstrated by the Oracle of Omaha himself.

5.3 Implementing Index Options

In our journey to understand and apply the strategies that have made Warren Buffett a legendary investor, we find ourselves at a crucial juncture—exploring the world of index options. Index options are an integral part of Buffett's investment toolkit, and they offer individual investors a unique avenue for optimizing their portfolios. In this sub-chapter, we'll delve deep into the practical aspects of implementing index options into your investment strategy.

Steps to Incorporate Index Options

To effectively incorporate index options into your investment strategy, it's imperative to follow a well-thought-out plan. The following steps will guide you on this path:

Step 1: Understand the Basics

Before diving into the world of index options, it's essential to have a firm grasp of the fundamentals. Understand what index options are, their types, and how they work. Take the time to learn the terminology, including terms like "calls" and "puts," and how they relate to options trading.

Step 2: Define Your Investment Objectives

Just as Warren Buffett emphasizes the importance of clear investment goals, you must define your own objectives.

What are you trying to achieve with index options? Are you looking to enhance returns, protect your portfolio during downturns, or both? Having a well-defined purpose will shape your options strategy.

Step 3: Choose the Right Index

Not all indexes are created equal, and your choice of underlying index matters. Consider factors such as the index's historical performance, volatility, and correlation with your existing holdings. Buffett often prefers options on broad market indexes like the S&P 500, as they provide diversification benefits.

Step 4: Determine Your Risk Tolerance

As with any investment strategy, understanding your risk tolerance is crucial. Options trading can be complex, and it involves the possibility of both gains and losses. Assess your willingness and ability to withstand fluctuations in your portfolio.

Step 5: Develop a Strategy

Based on your investment objectives and risk tolerance, develop a clear options strategy. Will you primarily buy calls or puts, or will you engage in more advanced strategies like covered calls or protective puts? Your choice should align with your goals.

Step 6: Execute Your Trades

Once you've formulated your strategy, it's time to execute your trades. Open an options trading account with a reputable broker, ensure you have the necessary approvals, and place your orders. Buffett often stresses the importance of low transaction costs, so be mindful of fees and commissions.

Risks and Mitigations

While index options offer attractive opportunities, they also come with inherent risks. Understanding these risks and implementing mitigations is essential to a successful options strategy:

Risk 1: Limited Duration

Options contracts have expiration dates, which means your strategy must adhere to a specific timeline. If the market doesn't move in your favor within the contract period, you could face losses. To mitigate this risk, consider longer-dated options that provide more time for your thesis to play out.

Risk 2: Volatility

Options prices are influenced by market volatility. Higher volatility can lead to increased options premiums, making them more expensive. You can mitigate this risk by carefully selecting entry and exit points and by diversifying your options positions.

Risk 3: Lack of Liquidity

Not all options contracts have the same level of liquidity. Some may have wide bid-ask spreads, making it challenging to enter and exit positions at favorable prices. Stick to actively traded options with tight spreads to minimize this risk.

Risk 4: Unforeseen Market Events

No strategy is immune to unexpected market events, such as economic crises or geopolitical turmoil. While you can't predict these events, you can protect your portfolio by maintaining a diversified approach and avoiding overexposure to options.

Monitoring and Adjusting Your Options Strategy

Once you've implemented your index options strategy, your work doesn't end there. Just as Warren Buffett continually monitors his investments, you must vigilantly oversee your options positions. Here's how to effectively monitor and adjust your strategy:

Regularly Review Your Portfolio

Set aside time for periodic reviews of your portfolio. Assess how your options positions are performing and whether they align with your investment objectives. Look for any changes in market conditions that may necessitate adjustments.

Stay Informed

Stay informed about developments in the market, economic indicators, and news that may impact your options positions. Buffett's success is grounded in his deep understanding of the companies he invests in—similarly, you should have a comprehensive understanding of your options strategy.

Use Risk Management Tools

Consider employing risk management tools like stop-loss orders or position sizing to limit potential losses. Buffett is known for his emphasis on capital preservation, and these tools can help protect your capital.

Adjust Strategically

As market conditions change, be prepared to adjust your options strategy accordingly. This might involve closing out positions that are no longer aligned with your goals or rolling options to a different expiration date.

Incorporating index options into your investment strategy can be a powerful tool for optimizing returns and managing risk, mirroring the approach of the Oracle of Omaha himself. However, it's essential to approach options with caution, understanding the nuances and risks involved. By following these steps and implementing robust risk management, you can effectively navigate the world of index options and enhance your potential for success in the investing game.

Part III: Building Your Investment Strategy

Chapter 6: Risk Management

6.1 The Importance of Risk Management

Risk—the ever-present shadow in the world of investing. It's a subject that even the most seasoned investors cannot afford to overlook. While the allure of high returns and the excitement of market rallies may be the siren's call for many, it is prudent risk management that separates successful investors from the rest. In this chapter, we'll delve deep into the art and science of risk management, a subject close to Warren Buffett's heart, and explore why it should be at the core of every investor's strategy.

The Role of Risk in Investing

Before we embark on understanding how to manage risk, it's imperative to acknowledge its fundamental role in investing. Risk, in essence, is the possibility of losing some or all of your investment. It's the turbulent undercurrent beneath the seemingly calm surface of financial markets. Contrary to the whimsical notion that one can eliminate risk altogether, the truth is that risk is an integral part of the investment landscape.

Warren Buffett himself has never advocated the avoidance of risk. Rather, he emphasizes understanding and managing it. This aligns with the famous adage: "It's not whether you're right or wrong that's important, but how much money you make when you're right and how much you lose when you're wrong." Risk, therefore, isn't a foe to be defeated but a force to be harnessed.

Buffett's investment philosophy revolves around seeking opportunities with an adequate margin of safety. It's about identifying investments where the potential for reward significantly outweighs the risk. This is where risk management takes center stage. It's the compass that guides investors through turbulent waters towards the shores of financial prosperity.

Buffett's Approach to Risk

Warren Buffett's approach to risk is marked by a blend of prudence and patience. He doesn't view risk in isolation but rather in the context of the potential rewards. He's known for his mantra: "Rule No. 1: Never lose money. Rule No. 2: Never forget Rule No. 1." This underscores his commitment to capital preservation.

One of the key ways Buffett manages risk is by investing in businesses he truly understands. He's often said that the best investment you can make is in yourself—through education. By deeply comprehending the businesses he invests in, he reduces the risk associated with making ill-informed decisions.

Furthermore, Buffett approaches risk with a long-term perspective. He is unfazed by short-term market fluctuations and remains committed to his investments through thick and thin. His steadfastness is a testament to the importance of time in risk management. Time, after all, is a potent ally in the world of investing. It allows compounding to work its magic and can mitigate the impact of market volatility.

How to Protect Your Investments

The importance of protecting your investments cannot be overstated. It's a facet of risk management that is often overshadowed by the allure of returns. But without adequate protection, your hard-earned gains can swiftly dissipate in the face of unforeseen events.

One of the primary ways to safeguard your investments is through diversification. Buffett himself has emphasized the importance of not putting all your eggs in one basket. Diversification involves spreading your investments across various asset classes, industries, and geographic regions. By doing so, you reduce the risk associated with the underperformance of a single investment.

Another crucial aspect of protecting your investments is maintaining an emergency fund. This is a cash reserve set aside for unexpected expenses or emergencies. It serves as a financial cushion, preventing you from having to liquidate your investments at an inopportune time to cover unforeseen costs.

Insurance also plays a pivotal role in risk management. It provides a safety net in the event of unforeseen disasters, be it health, property, or liability insurance. While insurance may not directly boost your investment returns, it shields your financial well-being from catastrophic events.

Lastly, continuous monitoring your investment portfolio are essential practices in risk management. As market conditions evolve, the risk-return profile of your investments may change. Regular assessment and adjustment ensure that your portfolio aligns with your risk tolerance and investment goals.

Risk management is the guardian of your financial future. Warren Buffett's success is a testament to the importance of not shying away from risk but rather understanding it, managing it, and harnessing it to achieve your investment objectives. By acknowledging the role of risk, adopting Buffett's approach, and implementing prudent protective measures, you fortify your position as an investor, ensuring that the road ahead is not only profitable but also safeguarded against the uncertainties that inevitably arise in the world of investing.

6.2 Diversification and Asset Allocation

Risk is the ever-present antagonist. It lurks in the shadows, ready to pounce when you least expect it. If there's one paramount lesson we can glean from the sage, Warren Buffett, it's that managing risk is not an afterthought; it's the cornerstone of sustainable wealth creation. While there is no foolproof shield against market volatility, there is a strategy that acts as a formidable guardian – diversification and asset allocation.

Diversifying Your Portfolio

Diversification is, in essence, the act of spreading your investments across a range of different assets. It's a bit like not putting all your eggs in one basket. The idea behind diversification is straightforward yet profound: by investing in a variety of asset classes, you can reduce the impact of a poor-performing investment on your overall portfolio.

Imagine you have a portfolio entirely composed of technology stocks. While tech stocks can deliver impressive returns during a bull market, they can also be particularly volatile. A single piece of bad news or a market correction can lead to significant losses. However, if you diversify your holdings by including bonds, real estate, and perhaps some commodities, you reduce your exposure to the ups and downs of the tech sector. When one asset class lags, others may rise, mitigating the overall impact on your portfolio.

Diversification doesn't guarantee profit or eliminate risk, but it helps manage risk. It's a strategy that aims to balance risk and reward by spreading your investments across different areas of the market. It's a bit like having a collection of different tools in your financial toolkit, each serving a specific purpose.

The Value of Asset Allocation

Diversification is only part of the equation. Asset allocation is the complementary strategy that guides how much of your portfolio should be invested in each asset class. It's the art of creating the right blend of investments to achieve your financial goals while managing risk.

Consider a novice sailor setting out to sea. To navigate effectively, they must determine the ideal mix of sails to harness the wind's power while keeping the boat steady. Similarly, asset allocation is about finding the right mix of assets to harness their potential for growth and income while maintaining the stability of your portfolio.

Asset allocation takes into account your investment objectives, risk tolerance, and time horizon. For instance, a young investor with a long time horizon may opt for a more aggressive allocation, with a higher proportion of equities, as they have time to ride out market fluctuations. In contrast, an investor approaching retirement might opt for a more conservative allocation, emphasizing income-producing assets and capital preservation.

Warren Buffett himself has emphasized the importance of asset allocation. His rule of thumb is to put 10% of the cash in short-term government bonds and 90% in a very low-cost S&P 500 index fund. This simple yet effective allocation strategy has been lauded for its ability to deliver solid returns while minimizing risk.

Building a Resilient Portfolio

A resilient portfolio is one that can withstand the challenges that inevitably arise in the financial markets. It's not about avoiding all losses—no strategy can promise that—but rather about preparing for them intelligently and minimizing their impact.

Building a resilient portfolio begins with a clear understanding of your financial goals and risk tolerance. It's about knowing how much volatility you can endure without losing sleep at night. Once you've established your objectives, diversification and asset allocation become the tools to sculpt your investment strategy.

An ideal portfolio is one that balances the pursuit of growth with the need for stability. It should be diversified across various asset classes, such as equities, bonds, real estate, and perhaps alternative investments like commodities or hedge funds. Each of these asset classes has its own risk-return profile, and by blending them strategically, you can aim for a smoother ride on the often turbulent seas of the financial markets.

Moreover, a resilient portfolio is not a static entity; it evolves over time. Market conditions change, economic landscapes shift, and personal circumstances evolve. Regularly revisiting your asset allocation to ensure it remains aligned with your goals and risk tolerance is a prudent practice.

Diversification and asset allocation are the bedrock of a sound investment strategy. These principles, championed by the likes of Warren Buffett, are the tools that allow investors to navigate the complex and unpredictable world of finance with confidence. By diversifying your investments and allocating your assets wisely, you can build a portfolio that not only pursues your financial goals but also weathers the storms that inevitably come your way.

6.3 Staying Calm During Market Turbulence

The turbulence of financial markets is an ever-present reality, and how we navigate this tempest can make all the difference between success and despair. In this sub-chapter, we shall delve into the emotional aspect of investing, discuss the importance of setting clear investment rules, examine Warren Buffett's emotional discipline, and explore strategies to maintain one's composure during volatile markets.

The Emotional Aspect of Investing

Investing isn't merely a financial endeavor; it's an emotional one as well. The rollercoaster ride of the stock market can trigger a cascade of emotions, from the euphoria of gains to the gut-wrenching fear of losses. Understanding these emotions and learning to manage them is a critical aspect of successful investing.

Firstly, there's the potent allure of greed. When markets are bullish, and stock prices are on an upward trajectory, it's easy to become intoxicated by the prospect of wealth. Investors may throw caution to the wind, chasing after hot stocks with little regard for fundamentals. This form of irrational exuberance can lead to speculative bubbles and, ultimately, painful corrections.

Conversely, there's the crushing weight of fear. During market downturns, panic can set in as portfolios hemorrhage value. Investors may be tempted to sell at the worst possible moment, locking in losses and missing out on potential recoveries. This fear-driven decision-making can be detrimental to long-term wealth accumulation.

Buffett himself is no stranger to these emotions. He's seen the markets soar to dizzying heights and crash to disheartening lows. Yet, he's remained steadfast in his approach, unwavering in the face of these emotional tempests.

Setting Clear Investment Rules

To navigate the stormy seas of investing, it's imperative to establish a set of clear and unyielding investment rules. These rules act as a compass, guiding us through turbulent times and ensuring that we don't stray too far from our intended course.

Buffett's investment rules are well-documented and offer invaluable insights for those seeking to emulate his success. One of his cardinal rules is never to invest in something you don't understand. This is akin to saying, "Don't sail into uncharted waters." By staying within your circle of competence, you reduce the risk of making rash decisions based on incomplete information.

Another of Buffett's rules is to be patient and disciplined. He often remarks that the stock market is a device for transferring money from the impatient to the patient. By setting rules that mandate a long-term horizon, you're less likely to succumb to the emotional rollercoaster of short-term market fluctuations.

Furthermore, diversification is a central tenet of Buffett's investment strategy. Diversification spreads risk and helps mitigate the impact of individual stock volatility. This rule acts as a lifeboat, protecting your portfolio from being swamped by a single investment's troubles.

Buffett's Emotional Discipline

Warren Buffett is renowned for his emotional discipline in the face of market turbulence. While others may panic and sell in a downturn, Buffett often seizes the opportunity to buy quality stocks at discounted prices. His emotional resilience is rooted in his unwavering belief in the long-term prospects of the businesses he invests in.

One of the ways Buffett maintains emotional discipline is by staying well-informed. He doesn't make investment decisions based on gut feelings but rather on a deep understanding of the companies he invests in. This knowledge provides him with the confidence to weather short-term storms, secure in the knowledge that quality will prevail over time.

Additionally, Buffett adheres to a value investing approach. He looks for stocks that are undervalued by the market, offering a margin of safety. This approach provides a cushion during market downturns, helping to alleviate emotional stress.

Strategies to Stay Calm During Volatile Markets
In the heat of market turbulence, it can be challenging to maintain one's composure. However, adopting a few key strategies can help you navigate these tempestuous waters with poise.

Firstly, embrace the power of knowledge. Educate yourself about the market, the assets you're invested in, and the factors that drive their performance. Knowledge is a powerful antidote to fear and uncertainty.

Secondly, have a plan in place. Your investment plan should outline your long-term goals, risk tolerance, and strategies for various market scenarios. When volatility strikes, refer to your plan as a source of reassurance and guidance.

Thirdly, avoid the temptation to check your portfolio constantly. Buffett himself famously remarked that the stock market is designed to transfer money from the impatient to the patient. Constantly monitoring your investments can lead to impulsive decisions based on short-term fluctuations.

Lastly, seek the counsel of a trusted financial advisor. Having a professional by your side can provide an objective perspective and prevent you from making emotionally charged decisions.

Staying calm during market turbulence is a hallmark of successful investors like Warren Buffett. Emotions are an inherent part of investing, but by understanding them, setting clear rules, and maintaining emotional discipline, you can weather the storms and navigate towards your financial goals with confidence and resilience.

Chapter 7: Crafting Your Investment Plan

7.1 Setting Clear Investment Goals

In the journey to win like Warren Buffett in the world of investing, one of the foundational steps, and indeed, a cornerstone of a successful strategy, is the careful crafting of your investment plan. At its heart, your investment plan is a roadmap, a guiding light that illuminates your path through the sometimes uncertain terrain of financial markets. In this sub-chapter, we will embark on the first leg of this journey, a leg that involves setting clear investment goals.

Defining Your Financial Objectives

Before venturing forth, it's imperative to know where you're headed. In the realm of investments, this translates into having a clear understanding of your financial objectives. Your objectives are essentially the destinations on your investment roadmap, the places you aspire to reach.

To define your financial objectives, you must ask yourself fundamental questions. What do you wish to achieve through your investments? Are you aiming for financial independence, seeking to fund your children's education, or perhaps planning for a comfortable retirement? These objectives are deeply personal, and there's no one-size-fits-all answer.

Here, we find a connection with Warren Buffett's own approach. While he is celebrated for his shrewd investment decisions, his success is underpinned by the clarity of his objectives. His primary goal has always been long-term wealth preservation and growth for Berkshire Hathaway shareholders. By establishing a clear objective, Buffett aligns his investment decisions with this overarching aim.

Short-term vs. Long-term Goals

The road to financial success in investing can be long and winding. Along the way, you will encounter various opportunities and challenges. To navigate effectively, it's crucial to differentiate between short-term and long-term goals.

Short-term goals typically have a horizon of one to three years. They might encompass saving for a down payment on a house, taking a dream vacation, or paying off high-interest debt. These goals require a more conservative investment approach, prioritizing capital preservation and liquidity.

Long-term goals, on the other hand, extend beyond three years and often span decades. Retirement planning, creating generational wealth, or building a significant investment portfolio are examples of long-term goals. These objectives allow for a more aggressive investment stance, as they have the luxury of time to ride out market fluctuations.

Buffett, renowned for his steadfast commitment to a long-term perspective, exemplifies this principle. His investment horizon stretches years, even decades, aligning with his objective of enduring wealth creation. He views market volatility not as a threat but as an opportunity, knowing that in the long run, well-chosen investments tend to appreciate significantly.

Aligning Your Goals with Your Risk Tolerance
With your financial objectives set, the next crucial step is aligning them with your risk tolerance. Risk tolerance is a deeply personal aspect of investing and reflects your willingness and ability to endure market fluctuations without making impulsive decisions.

Warren Buffett's risk tolerance is famously characterized by his stoic temperament. He remains unruffled in the face of market turbulence, which is a testament to his risk tolerance. His willingness to withstand short-term losses in pursuit of long-term gains is a hallmark of his success.

Your risk tolerance is your ability and willingness to withstand fluctuations in the value of your investments. It's influenced by factors such as your investment horizon, financial capacity to absorb losses, and your emotional temperament.

Here's where the art of investing meets the science. Your risk tolerance should harmonize with your financial objectives. If your goals are primarily short-term and you have a low tolerance for risk, your portfolio should reflect this by emphasizing capital preservation. Conversely, if your objectives are long-term and you can stomach short-term market volatility, you might consider a more growth-oriented approach.

A critical factor to consider is your emotional temperament. How do you react when markets take a downturn? Do you lose sleep over short-term losses, or can you maintain a long-term perspective? Understanding your emotional responses to market movements will help you tailor your investment strategy to suit your psychological comfort zone.

Remember, there's no one-size-fits-all approach to risk tolerance. It's a deeply personal aspect of investing. What's most important is that your portfolio aligns with both your financial objectives and your ability to withstand the inevitable market ups and downs.

Setting clear investment goals is the foundation of a successful investing journey. It involves defining your financial objectives, distinguishing between short-term and long-term goals, and aligning these goals with your risk tolerance. Your objectives will shape your investment strategy, guiding you toward achieving your financial dreams.

7.2 Designing Your Portfolio

In the world of investing, crafting an effective and resilient investment plan is akin to constructing a sturdy and reliable foundation for a building. The strength and durability of your portfolio depend significantly on the thoughtfulness and precision with which you design it. This sub-chapter delves deep into the art of designing your portfolio, examining asset allocation strategies, diversification techniques, and the delicate balance between risk and return.

Asset Allocation Strategies

Asset allocation is the bedrock upon which your investment portfolio rests. It is the art of spreading your investments across different asset classes, such as stocks, bonds, and cash equivalents, in a deliberate and strategic manner. The goal here is not just to allocate your assets but to do so in a way that aligns with your financial objectives, risk tolerance, and investment horizon.

Warren Buffett, the sage of Omaha, often emphasizes the importance of asset allocation. He contends that it is not about timing the market but rather time in the market that matters. Buffett's approach to asset allocation is characterized by a significant allocation to equities, particularly high-quality, dividend-paying stocks. This allocation provides the potential for long-term growth, which has been the cornerstone of his investment success.

However, the key to asset allocation is not one-size-fits-all. It must be tailored to your unique financial situation and goals. Here are three fundamental asset allocation strategies to consider:

1. Aggressive Growth Allocation: This strategy involves a higher allocation to stocks, typically around 80-90% of your portfolio. It is suited for investors with a long time horizon, a high tolerance for risk, and a desire for substantial capital appreciation. This strategy aligns closely with Warren Buffett's approach and can deliver impressive returns over time.

2. Balanced Allocation: A balanced approach involves a mix of stocks and bonds, usually in a 60-40 or 70-30 ratio. It provides a reasonable compromise between growth and stability. Investors who want to capture some market upside while mitigating risk often favor this strategy. It aligns well with the idea of preserving capital during market downturns.

3. Conservative Allocation: For investors who prioritize capital preservation and income generation, a conservative allocation may be suitable. This strategy involves a significant allocation to bonds, with a smaller portion allocated to stocks. It's a strategy that suits those with a shorter investment horizon and lower risk tolerance, such as retirees.

Your asset allocation should be a dynamic and evolving aspect of your investment plan. Regular reviews and adjustments are essential to ensure that your portfolio remains aligned with your goals and risk tolerance as your financial circumstances change.

Diversification Techniques

Diversification is a fundamental concept that goes hand in hand with asset allocation. It is the strategy of spreading your investments within each asset class to reduce risk. The idea is to avoid putting all your eggs in one basket, thereby minimizing the impact of a poor-performing investment on your overall portfolio.

Warren Buffett himself is an advocate of diversification, albeit with a twist. He famously said, "Diversification is protection against ignorance. It makes little sense if you know what you are doing." This statement underscores the importance of understanding your investments thoroughly.

However, for common investors who may not have Buffett's level of expertise, diversification remains a vital risk management tool. Here are some diversification techniques to consider:

1. Asset Class Diversification: As mentioned earlier, this involves spreading your investments across different asset classes, such as stocks, bonds, real estate, and cash equivalents. Each asset class reacts differently to economic conditions, providing a hedge against volatility.

2. Geographic Diversification: Beyond asset classes, consider diversifying your investments across geographic regions and markets. Investing solely in one country or region exposes your portfolio to local economic and geopolitical risks. By branching out globally, you can reduce these risks.

3. Sector Diversification: Within the stock portion of your portfolio, diversify further by investing in various sectors of the economy, such as technology, healthcare, consumer goods, and energy. Different sectors perform differently under varying economic conditions, contributing to your portfolio's stability.

4. Individual Security Diversification: If you invest in individual stocks, aim for a well-diversified portfolio of individual securities. Avoid overconcentration in a single stock or industry, as this can lead to substantial risk. Buffett himself has advocated for a concentrated portfolio of his best ideas, but for the average investor, diversification can be a prudent approach.

5. Time Diversification: Invest regularly over time, regardless of market conditions. This strategy, often referred to as dollar-cost averaging, helps you avoid trying to time the market and reduces the impact of market volatility on your investments.

Balancing Risk and Return

The delicate balance between risk and return is at the heart of portfolio design. The relationship is akin to a seesaw, where increasing one side usually results in a decrease in the other. Common investors often grapple with finding this equilibrium, and it's an area where Warren Buffett's wisdom can guide our approach.

Buffett's investment philosophy emphasizes two critical aspects: a focus on the long term and a preference for high-quality assets. These principles naturally influence how we strike the balance between risk and return in our portfolios.

When designing your portfolio, consider the following principles to achieve that balance:

1. Risk Assessment: Begin by assessing your risk tolerance. How much volatility can you comfortably endure without making rash decisions? Understand that risk is not just about losing money but also the emotional toll it can take.

2. Investment Horizon: Your time horizon is a crucial factor in determining your risk-return profile. Buffett's success is largely attributed to his long-term perspective. Align your investments with your financial goals and the time it will take to achieve them.

3. Quality Over Quantity: Like Buffett, prioritize high-quality investments over high-risk, speculative ones. Focus on businesses with strong competitive advantages, consistent earnings, and reliable dividend histories. Quality assets tend to offer a more stable path to wealth accumulation.

4. Dollar-Cost Averaging: Avoid trying to time the market and make large lump-sum investments. Instead, employ a disciplined approach like dollar-cost averaging, which spreads your investments over time. This mitigates the risk of investing all your capital at a market peak.

5. Review and Rebalance: Regularly review your portfolio to ensure it remains aligned with your risk tolerance and

investment goals. Market fluctuations may cause your asset allocation to drift from its intended target, requiring rebalancing to restore the desired balance.

In the world of investing, risk is inevitable, but it can be managed and mitigated through thoughtful portfolio design. Striking the right balance between risk and return is a dynamic process that evolves as your financial circumstances and goals change. Warren Buffett's wisdom provides invaluable guidance in achieving this equilibrium and crafting a portfolio that stands the test of time.

Designing your portfolio is a crucial step in building a resilient investment plan. Asset allocation, diversification, and balancing risk and return are the cornerstones of this process. By applying these principles, you can construct a portfolio that aligns with your financial objectives, risk tolerance, and investment horizon, all while drawing inspiration from the wisdom of Warren Buffett. Remember, the journey to financial success is not a sprint but a marathon, and a well-designed portfolio will be your steadfast companion along the way.

7.3 Creating a Practical Investment Plan

In the realm of investing, the journey to financial success begins with a well-thought-out plan—a roadmap, if you will. Crafting a practical investment plan is akin to plotting a course for a long and arduous journey. It is not merely about selecting stocks or financial instruments; it encompasses a broader perspective that includes goal setting, risk assessment, asset allocation, and an unwavering commitment to a disciplined approach. In this sub-chapter, we will explore the essential components of creating a practical investment plan, each of which plays a crucial role in the realization of your financial aspirations.

Building Your Investment Roadmap

Before embarking on any journey, it is essential to know your destination. In the world of investing, your destination is your financial goal. Whether you seek to fund your child's education, build a retirement nest egg, or achieve financial independence, setting clear and realistic investment objectives is paramount.

Begin by defining your financial goals, both short-term and long-term. Understand the time horizon for each goal, as it will influence your investment strategy. Short-term goals, such as buying a house in the next five years, may require a more conservative approach, while long-term goals like retirement planning can afford a longer investment horizon.

Once your goals are defined, quantify them. Assign specific dollar values to your objectives. This not only provides clarity but also allows you to gauge your progress over time. Remember, a goal without a specific target is like a ship without a compass.

With your goals in place, it's time to assess your risk tolerance. Understand that risk is an inherent part of investing, and different individuals have varying levels of risk tolerance. Ask yourself how comfortable you are with market fluctuations and the possibility of losing some portion of your investment. Your risk tolerance will help determine the mix of assets in your portfolio.

Diversification is a core principle of risk management. It involves spreading your investments across various asset classes such as stocks, bonds, and real estate. Diversification reduces the impact of poor performance in any single asset class on your overall portfolio. Building an investment roadmap, therefore, requires careful consideration of asset allocation. The allocation should align with your goals and risk tolerance.

It is worth noting that your investment roadmap is not a static document. Life circumstances change, goals evolve, and market conditions fluctuate. Regularly review and, if necessary, adjust your investment plan. This adaptability ensures that your roadmap remains relevant and effective in helping you achieve your financial objectives.

Automating Your Investments

Now that you have your investment roadmap, it's time to execute your plan consistently. One of the most effective ways to do this is by automating your investments. Automation removes the emotional aspect of investing, which can often lead to impulsive decisions.

Start by setting up automatic contributions to your investment accounts. Whether it's a retirement account, brokerage account, or a dedicated savings account, automate regular deposits. This "pay yourself first" mentality ensures that your investments are a priority, not an afterthought.

Consider using dollar-cost averaging (DCA) as part of your automated investment strategy. With DCA, you invest a fixed amount of money at regular intervals, regardless of market conditions. This approach allows you to buy more shares when prices are low and fewer shares when prices are high, ultimately reducing the impact of market volatility on your portfolio.

Furthermore, take advantage of employer-sponsored retirement plans, like 401(k)s, if available. These plans often offer automatic payroll deductions and employer matching contributions, making it easy to save for retirement without even thinking about it.

Remember, consistency in investing pays dividends over time. By automating your investments, you create a habit that can lead to long-term financial success.

Monitoring and Adjusting Your Plan
A well-crafted investment plan is not a "set it and forget it" proposition. Markets are dynamic, and your financial circumstances may change. Regular monitoring and adjustment of your plan are essential to staying on course.

Start by establishing a routine for reviewing your portfolio. This can be quarterly, semi-annually, or annually, depending on your preferences and the complexity of your investments. During these reviews, assess the performance of your portfolio against your goals. Are you on track to meet your objectives? If not, adjustments may be necessary.

When making adjustments, avoid knee-jerk reactions to short-term market fluctuations. Instead, base your decisions on your long-term goals and risk tolerance. If you find that your asset allocation has deviated from your intended targets, rebalance your portfolio to realign it with your original plan.

Life events can also trigger the need for plan adjustments. Significant changes such as marriage, the birth of a child, a job change, or an unexpected windfall should prompt a reevaluation of your investment strategy. These events may require modifications to your asset allocation, risk tolerance, or financial goals.

Additionally, stay informed about changes in tax laws, economic conditions, and investment trends that may impact your portfolio. Seek professional guidance when necessary, and don't hesitate to consult with a financial advisor who can provide expert insights and assist you in making informed decisions.

Creating a practical investment plan is the foundation of a successful financial journey. It begins with setting clear goals and understanding your risk tolerance, followed by careful asset allocation and the automation of investments. However, remember that your plan should remain adaptable and subject to regular review and adjustment. With dedication, discipline, and a well-structured investment plan, you can navigate the complex landscape of investing and work towards achieving your financial aspirations.

Chapter 8: Building a Befitting Portfolio

8.1 Modern Portfolio Theory (MPT)

In the realm of investment, the Modern Portfolio Theory (MPT) stands as a testament to the power of rigorous analysis and mathematical precision. Developed by Harry Markowitz in the early 1950s, this theory has had a profound impact on the way investors approach portfolio construction. In this chapter, we will delve into the intricacies of MPT, exploring its key components: diversification benefits, the concept of the efficient frontier, and how you can practically apply MPT principles to construct a portfolio that befits your financial goals.

Diversification Benefits

Diversification is a concept so ingrained in the fabric of modern finance that its importance cannot be overstated. At its core, diversification involves spreading your investments across different asset classes or securities to reduce risk. In the world of MPT, risk is not synonymous with return. Instead, it is defined as the volatility or variability of returns.

The rationale behind diversification is simple yet profound. By investing in a variety of assets that don't move in perfect synchrony, you can mitigate the impact of poor performance in one area with potentially better performance in another. Think of it as a safety net for your investments.

Diversification benefits are rooted in the idea that assets react differently to economic events and market conditions. When you combine assets with low or negative correlations, you create a portfolio that can weather various market storms. For instance, during economic downturns, traditionally safer assets like bonds may rise in value while stocks decline. In contrast, when the economy is booming, stocks may soar while bond returns remain steady.

One of the essential principles of MPT is that, through diversification, you can reduce the overall risk of your portfolio without necessarily sacrificing returns. By carefully selecting a mix of assets, you can achieve a more favorable risk-return profile.

The Efficient Frontier
To understand the concept of the efficient frontier, imagine a graph with risk on the x-axis and expected return on the y-axis. Each point on this graph represents a different portfolio, each with its unique combination of assets. Some portfolios will offer higher returns but at the cost of higher risk, while others may provide lower returns with lower risk.

The efficient frontier is a curve that traces the optimal combination of assets for the given level of risk. Portfolios along this curve are considered efficient because they offer the highest expected return for a specific level of risk or the lowest risk for a given level of expected return. In essence, it showcases the sweet spot where investors can maximize returns while minimizing risk.

The concept of the efficient frontier highlights a critical aspect of portfolio management: risk is inherent, but it should be compensated with higher expected returns. It also underscores the trade-off that investors face between risk and reward. To achieve higher returns, one must be willing to accept a commensurate increase in risk.

Applying MPT to Construct Your Portfolio
Now, let's bridge the theory of MPT with the practicalities of constructing a portfolio that aligns with your financial goals and risk tolerance. The essence of MPT is to find the right mix of assets that provides the highest expected return for your acceptable level of risk.

1. Asset Allocation: The first step in applying MPT is to determine your asset allocation. This involves deciding how much of your portfolio will be allocated to different asset classes such as stocks, bonds, and potentially alternative investments like real estate or commodities. Your allocation should reflect your financial goals, investment horizon, and risk tolerance.

   - Key Point 1: Define Your Financial Goals: Begin by setting clear financial objectives. Are you investing for retirement, education, or a major purchase? Your goals will influence your time horizon and risk tolerance.

   - Key Point 2: Assess Your Risk Tolerance: Understand your willingness and ability to tolerate risk. Consider factors like your age, investment experience, and emotional temperament when faced with market volatility.

- Key Point 3: Diversify Across Asset Classes: Diversify your portfolio by allocating assets across different classes. MPT suggests that a diversified portfolio can provide better risk-adjusted returns.

2. Security Selection: Once you've determined your asset allocation, the next step is to select specific securities or funds within each asset class. This involves careful research and analysis to identify investments that align with your goals and risk profile.

- Key Point 1: Research and Due Diligence: Conduct thorough research on individual securities or funds. Consider factors such as historical performance, fees, management, and alignment with your investment objectives.

- Key Point 2: Monitor and Rebalance: Regularly review your portfolio to ensure it stays aligned with your target asset allocation. Over time, market movements may cause your portfolio to drift from its intended mix.

- Key Point 3: Avoid Emotional Decision-Making: Emotions can lead to impulsive decisions that undermine your long-term strategy. Stick to your investment plan, even during periods of market turbulence.

3. Risk Management: While MPT can help you build a portfolio with an optimal risk-return trade-off, it's essential to continually manage and mitigate risk.

- Key Point 1: Diversification Across Assets: Diversification is a cornerstone of risk management. Spread your investments across various assets to reduce the impact of poor-performing securities.

- Key Point 2: Rebalancing: Regularly rebalance your portfolio to maintain your desired asset allocation. This ensures that your risk exposure stays in line with your objectives.

- Key Point 3: Stay Informed: Stay informed about changes in the financial markets and the economy. Awareness of economic indicators and market trends can help you make informed decisions.

In the world of investing, Modern Portfolio Theory offering a systematic approach to building portfolios that aim to optimize returns while managing risk. By understanding the benefits of diversification, recognizing the concept of the efficient frontier, and applying MPT principles to construct your portfolio, you can navigate the complex landscape of investments with confidence and purpose.

8.2 Alternative Investments

In the quest for building a well-rounded portfolio that stands the test of time, the savvy investor often treads beyond the familiar terrain of stocks and bonds. In this sub-chapter, we embark on a journey into the realm of alternative investments, a world where traditional assets meet non-traditional possibilities. Exploring these non-conventional avenues can add depth and resilience to your investment portfolio, but it's a path laden with both unique opportunities and distinctive risks. Let's delve deeper into the realm of alternative investments, understanding their significance, and weighing the pros and cons of venturing into this uncharted territory.

Exploring Non-Traditional Assets

Traditional investments, such as stocks and bonds, are the bedrock of most portfolios. However, alternative investments encompass a wide range of asset classes that extend well beyond these conventional options. Non-traditional assets include real assets like real estate and commodities, hedge funds, private equity, venture capital, and even cryptocurrencies.

The allure of non-traditional assets lies in their potential to generate returns that are uncorrelated or less correlated with traditional markets. This means that when traditional investments zig, alternative investments may zag. This can be a valuable attribute during times of market turbulence, as these assets may provide diversification benefits and act as a hedge against economic downturns.

Real Assets and Their Role in Diversification

Real assets, such as real estate and commodities, have been a cornerstone of alternative investments. Real estate, in particular, has long been favored by investors seeking income generation and capital appreciation. The physical nature of real estate offers a tangible asset that can provide stability in a portfolio. Properties can generate rental income, and their value tends to appreciate over the long term, making them attractive options for those looking to diversify beyond stocks and bonds.

Commodities, on the other hand, offer exposure to tangible goods like gold, oil, and agricultural products. Investing in commodities can be a strategic move to hedge against inflation, as these assets often retain their value in times of rising prices. Additionally, commodities can behave differently from traditional financial assets, further enhancing portfolio diversification.

The Pros and Cons of Alternative Investments

Before venturing into alternative investments, it's essential to weigh the advantages and disadvantages of these options carefully.

Pros:

1. Diversification: One of the primary advantages of alternative investments is their potential to diversify your portfolio. Their returns often have a low correlation with traditional assets, which means that when stocks and bonds

are underperforming, alternative investments may provide stability.

2. Potential for Higher Returns: Some alternative investments, such as venture capital and private equity, offer the opportunity for substantial returns. These investments often involve backing early-stage companies with significant growth potential.

3. Inflation Hedge: Assets like real estate and commodities can serve as effective hedges against inflation. As the prices of goods and services rise, the value of these tangible assets tends to increase, preserving your purchasing power.

Cons:

1. Lack of Liquidity: Alternative investments, such as private equity and venture capital, are typically illiquid. Your capital may be tied up for an extended period, making it challenging to access in case of unexpected financial needs.

2. Complexity and Risk: Many alternative investments come with higher complexity and risk. Understanding the intricacies of these assets and conducting thorough due diligence is crucial. Additionally, some alternative investments, like hedge funds, may charge higher fees than traditional investments.

3. Regulatory Considerations: Regulations surrounding alternative investments can be intricate, and they may vary depending on your location. Complying with these

regulations and ensuring your investments are structured appropriately is essential.

Alternative investments can be a valuable addition to your portfolio, offering diversification benefits and the potential for enhanced returns. However, they come with their own set of complexities and risks. Before delving into the world of alternative investments, it's advisable to consult with a financial advisor who can help you navigate this terrain effectively. When approached with diligence and a clear understanding of their role in your portfolio, alternative investments can contribute to the construction of a portfolio that not only weathers the storms but also thrives in diverse market conditions.

8.3 Dynamic Asset Allocation

In the world of investing, change is the only constant. Market dynamics, economic conditions, and individual goals all evolve over time. To stay ahead in the investing game, one must master the art of dynamic asset allocation. In this sub-chapter, we'll delve into the intricacies of adjusting your portfolio over time, implementing effective rebalancing strategies, and the importance of regular portfolio reviews.

Adjusting Your Portfolio Over Time

Warren Buffett's investment philosophy is not etched in stone. It's a living, breathing approach that adapts to the ever-changing financial landscape. As common investors, we must recognize the need for flexibility in our portfolios. But how does one go about adjusting a portfolio over time, especially in the context of Buffett's wisdom?

Evolution of Objectives

Your investment objectives are not static; they evolve as you progress through life. Early on, your focus may be on growth and capital accumulation. As life unfolds, the need for income and wealth preservation may take center stage. Buffett's teachings emphasize the importance of aligning your investments with your objectives. Regularly reassess and adjust your portfolio to reflect your changing financial goals.

Asset Allocation Rebalancing

Dynamic asset allocation involves periodic reassessment and realignment of your portfolio's asset mix. As markets fluctuate, your asset allocation may drift from its original targets. To bring it back in line, consider rebalancing. Buffett's approach, rooted in patience, doesn't mean ignoring market realities. Rebalancing is a strategy that marries his long-term focus with the necessity of adjusting to current conditions.

Tax Efficiency

Buffett is known for his tax-efficient investment strategies. When adjusting your portfolio, consider the tax implications of your actions. Are there opportunities to minimize capital gains taxes? Can you offset gains with losses? Buffett's careful consideration of tax consequences is a vital aspect of his approach. Pay attention to tax-efficient strategies to maximize returns while minimizing liabilities.

Rebalancing Strategies

Rebalancing is the art of restoring your portfolio to its original asset allocation targets. It ensures that risk and return profiles remain aligned with your objectives. In Buffett's world, rebalancing is not about frenetic trading but about maintaining a steady course.

Setting Thresholds

Establishing thresholds is the cornerstone of effective rebalancing. Define a percentage range within which an asset class should fluctuate before taking action. For instance, if your target allocation for stocks is 60%, consider rebalancing when the stock portion of your portfolio moves beyond 65% or falls below 55%. This disciplined approach prevents overreactions to short-term market swings.

Asset Class Correlations

Buffett's wisdom extends to recognizing that different asset classes exhibit varying degrees of correlation. In rebalancing, take into account how asset classes interact with one another. If stocks and bonds have become highly correlated due to market conditions, rebalancing might necessitate a more substantial shift in your allocation strategy.

Regularity and Patience

Buffett's rebalancing strategy doesn't involve frequent, knee-jerk reactions to market movements. Instead, it advocates for a disciplined, periodic review and adjustment. Regularity in rebalancing ensures that your portfolio remains aligned with your long-term objectives. Resist the temptation to react impulsively to short-term market noise, and allow time for your strategic adjustments to bear fruit.

Portfolio Monitoring and Regular Reviews
In the world of value investing, patience is a virtue. However, it doesn't imply a lack of vigilance. Regularly monitoring your portfolio is akin to steering a ship on a steady course.

Tracking Performance Metrics

Buffett advises investors to keep a watchful eye on the performance of their investments. Understand the metrics that matter most to your portfolio. Is it beating the benchmark? How are individual holdings performing? Metrics such as return on equity (ROE) and price-to-earnings (P/E) ratios should be part of your regular assessment.

Adapting to Changing Conditions

Buffett's success is partly attributed to his ability to adapt to changing market conditions. As you monitor your portfolio, stay attuned to economic and market developments. Be prepared to adjust your asset allocation if macroeconomic factors demand it. Remember, staying the course doesn't mean ignoring reality; it means making well-informed, deliberate choices.

Learning from Mistakes and Successes

Warren Buffett often emphasizes the importance of learning from both your successes and your mistakes. Conduct post-mortems on investments that didn't pan out as expected. Conversely, analyze your successful investments to identify patterns and principles that led to positive outcomes. This iterative learning process is a hallmark of Buffett's approach.

Dynamic asset allocation is the cornerstone of a resilient portfolio. Emulating Warren Buffett's investment philosophy requires the ability to adapt, rebalance effectively, and maintain a vigilant watch over your investments. The essence of Buffett's wisdom lies not only in selecting the right stocks but also in managing your portfolio judiciously over time. As you navigate the dynamic world of investing, remember that patience, adaptability, and discipline will be your most valuable assets.

Chapter 9: The Long-Term Perspective

9.1 The Magic of Compounding

In the world of investing, there is a phenomenon that can only be described as magical. It's a force so powerful that it has the potential to turn modest savings into substantial wealth over time. This phenomenon is known as compounding, and it lies at the heart of Warren Buffett's long-term investment success. In this sub-chapter, we will unravel the mystery of compounding, explore its inner workings, and understand why it is such a potent force in the world of finance.

Understanding Compound Interest

Investing, at its core, is about making your money work for you. And when it comes to making your money work for you, there's no more powerful force at play than compound interest. It's a concept that Warren Buffett has not only understood but masterfully employed throughout his long and illustrious career. So, what exactly is compound interest?

At its core, compounding is a simple concept, yet its implications are profound. At its essence, it's about earning interest not just on your initial investment but also on the interest that your investment earns over time. To grasp the true power of compounding, let's consider a hypothetical scenario.

Imagine you invest $10,000 in a stock that generates an annual return of 10%. In the first year, you earn $1,000 in profit, bringing your total investment to $11,000. In the second year, you earn 10% on the new total, which is $1,100, not just on your initial $10,000. As time goes on, this cycle repeats, with your investment growing exponentially.

The key takeaway here is that as time progresses, the interest you earn starts to build upon itself, accelerating your investment growth. This is the essence of compound interest, and it's the force that has played a significant role in Warren Buffett's wealth accumulation.

Imagine you invest a sum of money. Over time, that initial investment generates returns. Now, here's where the magic happens. Those returns, in turn, generate their own returns. This cycle continues, and with each passing period, your wealth grows not just by addition but by multiplication. It's like a snowball rolling downhill, picking up more and more snow as it goes, becoming larger and more powerful.

The formula for compound interest is deceptively simple: $A = P(1 + r/n)^{(nt)}$. Here, "A" represents the final amount, "P" is the principal investment, "r" is the annual interest rate, "n" is the number of times that interest is compounded per year, and "t" is the number of years the money is invested. While the formula may seem complex, its implications are profound.

Buffett grasped this concept early in his career. He understood that the longer you leave your money invested, the more time it has to compound and grow exponentially. In essence, compound interest rewards the patient investor. Even small, consistent contributions to your investments can lead to substantial wealth over time. This is a cornerstone of Buffett's strategy and one of the secrets to his success.

The Power of Time

Time is an investor's most precious asset. It's a resource that, once spent, cannot be replenished. Warren Buffett recognized the significance of time from the outset of his investing journey. He started investing at a young age, and he's often said that his favorite holding period for a stock is "forever." Why? Because time allows for the full realization of the magic of compounding.

Consider two investors, one who starts investing at 25 and the other at 35. They both invest the same amount of money and earn the same annual return. However, the investor who starts at 25 will have a significantly larger nest egg by the time they reach retirement age. This is the influence of time at work.

Buffett's commitment to long-term investing is a testament to his understanding of the power of time. He isn't concerned with short-term market fluctuations or trying to time the market. Instead, he focuses on finding high-quality companies with enduring competitive advantages and holding them for the long haul. This patient approach has allowed him to benefit from the full potential of compound interest.

Moreover, time also provides the opportunity to weather market downturns and recover from setbacks. In the short term, markets can be unpredictable and volatile. But over the long term, they tend to trend upwards. By staying invested through the ups and downs, you harness the full power of time and compound interest to grow your wealth steadily and reliably.

How Buffett Benefits from the Long Term

Warren Buffett's investment success is a testament to the incredible rewards that patience and a long-term perspective can bring. He's famously held onto stocks like Coca-Cola and American Express for decades, reaping the benefits of compounding returns over time.

One of the most iconic examples of Buffett's long-term mindset is his investment in Berkshire Hathaway itself. When he took control of the struggling textile company in the 1960s, he transformed it into a diversified conglomerate. Over the years, Berkshire Hathaway's stock price has skyrocketed, turning the company into one of the most valuable in the world. Buffett's decision to hold onto his shares rather than cash out allowed him to accumulate enormous wealth through the power of time and compounding.

Buffett's approach to investing isn't about quick wins or chasing the latest fads. It's about finding solid businesses with competitive advantages, investing in them, and then having the patience to let them grow over many years. This strategy aligns perfectly with the principles of compound interest and the understanding that wealth creation is a marathon, not a sprint.

Understanding compound interest, appreciating the power of time, and embracing a long-term perspective are fundamental aspects of Warren Buffett's investment strategy. These principles have not only made him one of the most successful investors of all time but also serve as a guiding light for common investors looking to secure their financial futures. By following in Buffett's footsteps and harnessing the magic of compounding, you too can set yourself on a path to financial success and security.

9.2 Setting Realistic Goals

Setting and achieving financial goals is akin to plotting a course for a voyage across uncharted waters. It's a journey that demands clear direction, steady resolve, and, above all, an unwavering commitment to the long-term perspective—a perspective that has been central to Warren Buffett's remarkable success. In this sub-chapter, we will explore the pivotal role of setting realistic goals in your investment journey and how patience and progress tracking serve as your guiding stars.

Defining Your Financial Goals

The very essence of setting realistic goals in investing begins with an introspective exercise—defining your financial objectives. It's astonishing how often investors overlook this fundamental step, caught up in the excitement of markets and the allure of quick riches. Warren Buffett, however, exemplifies a different approach—a deliberate, methodical one that hinges on understanding one's financial aspirations.

Begin by asking yourself: What are you investing for? Is it your retirement, your children's education, or perhaps a dream vacation? Clearly defining your goals is akin to charting your destination on a nautical map. It not only provides a sense of purpose but also dictates your investment strategy.

Buffett's strategy, which thrives on long-term value creation, naturally aligns with the concept of well-defined goals. The Oracle of Omaha's primary goal was wealth preservation and steady growth over the long haul, which resonates with many investors looking to secure their financial future.

Consider this: If your aim is retirement, you must ascertain the desired age at which you wish to retire and the income you'd like to maintain during your retirement years. These specifics are the coordinates by which you navigate your investment ship. By having a precise destination in mind, you'll be better equipped to choose the investments and strategies that align with your goals.

Buffett's journey was equally purposeful. He didn't merely seek profits for the sake of it; his mission was to compound wealth consistently and sustainably. This clarity of purpose guided his investment decisions, anchoring them to his overarching financial goals.

The Role of Patience

With your financial goals in place, the next navigational tool at your disposal is patience—a virtue Buffett has in abundance. Patience, in the context of investing, entails the ability to withstand the ebb and flow of market turbulence while adhering steadfastly to your long-term objectives.

Picture this: As you embark on your voyage, you're bound to encounter unpredictable weather patterns. Similarly, in the world of investing, market fluctuations are as inevitable as the changing tides. Patience serves as your sturdy vessel, weathering the storms and providing the stability required to stay the course.

Warren Buffett's investment philosophy is steeped in patience. His mantra? Buy quality assets and hold them for the long term. This approach has enabled him to harness the magic of compounding—a force that amplifies returns over time. Buffett's journey is a testament to the rewards that come to those who steadfastly adhere to their chosen course.

For the common investor, it's essential to understand that market volatility, while unnerving, is but a part of the investment landscape. Buffett's unwavering patience during market downturns, such as the Great Recession of 2008, showcases the wisdom of enduring short-term setbacks for the sake of long-term gains. His ability to stay calm and collected amid market turmoil is a trait worth emulating.

To put it plainly, impatience can be the downfall of many an investor. The allure of quick profits can lead to impulsive decisions, often resulting in losses. Buffett, on

the other hand, exemplifies the power of restraint, which is
the linchpin of his remarkable success. Remember that
investing is not a sprint; it's a marathon—a journey that
demands steadfast patience to achieve your long-term
objectives.

Tracking Your Progress

As you navigate toward your financial goals, it's crucial to
keep a watchful eye on your progress—a practice often
overlooked in the whirlwind of market activity. Warren
Buffett, however, is renowned for his meticulous tracking
of investments, a habit that has contributed significantly to
his success.

Imagine sailing without instruments to monitor your
position, progress, and direction. In investing, the
equivalent of these instruments is tracking your portfolio's
performance. By regularly assessing how your investments
are faring, you can make informed decisions and adjust
your course as needed.

For Buffett, tracking progress involves a rigorous analysis
of his investments, coupled with an unwavering
commitment to learning from both successes and failures.
He maintains a comprehensive record of Berkshire
Hathaway's holdings, their performance, and the rationale
behind each investment—a practice that has served him
well over the years.

As a common investor, adopting this meticulous approach
may not require the same level of detail as Buffett, but it is

no less important. Regularly reviewing your investments allows you to identify underperforming assets, reevaluate your strategy, and make informed adjustments. Tracking progress is the compass that keeps you on course and ensures that you remain aligned with your financial goals.

Setting realistic financial goals, cultivating patience, and tracking your progress are fundamental aspects of the long-term perspective championed by Warren Buffett. Much like a seasoned navigator, Buffett has shown us that a clear destination, steady patience, and vigilant progress monitoring are essential elements of a successful investment journey. Embrace these principles, and you'll be well on your way to winning like Buffett in the investing game.

9.3 Wisdom from Successful Investors

In the realm of investing, the value of real-life success stories cannot be overstated. They serve as beacons of inspiration, offering insights into the journeys of those who have navigated the unpredictable waters of the financial markets and emerged victorious. Moreover, these stories provide invaluable lessons on the common pitfalls to avoid and emphasize the importance of continuous learning and growth.

Real-Life Success Stories

Investing is a journey filled with opportunities and challenges, and what better way to illustrate its intricacies than by examining the stories of successful investors? These individuals have traversed the treacherous terrain of financial markets and have emerged victorious. Their tales are not just inspiring but also contain valuable lessons for aspiring investors.

Success Story 1: Warren Buffett

At the heart of our discussion lies the remarkable success story of Warren Buffett, the Oracle of Omaha. Buffett's journey from a young boy with an affinity for numbers to one of the wealthiest individuals in the world is a testament to the power of disciplined investing.

Buffett's success is not just about amassing vast wealth but about doing so consistently over the long term. His philosophy of value investing, focusing on intrinsic value and economic moats, has proven time and again that patience, diligence, and sound decision-making can yield incredible results.

One key takeaway from Buffett's success is his unwavering commitment to his investment principles. He has shown that it's not about chasing the latest fads or market trends but about sticking to a well-thought-out strategy, even when it may not seem fashionable.

Success Story 2: Benjamin Graham

Another luminary in the world of investing is Benjamin Graham, often referred to as the "father of value investing." Graham's journey, chronicled in his book "The Intelligent Investor," serves as a guiding light for many investors.

Graham's early success was followed by a devastating setback during the Great Depression. However, he emerged from this experience with a renewed perspective on investing. He realized that true value investing required not just a focus on numbers but also a profound understanding of market psychology and the importance of emotional discipline.

Graham's success story emphasizes the significance of resilience in the face of adversity. It's a reminder that setbacks are part and parcel of investing, and it's how we respond to them that ultimately defines our success.

Success Story 3: Sir John Templeton

One such luminary is Sir John Templeton, a renowned investor who founded the Templeton Growth Fund in 1954. His story is a testament to the power of a contrarian mindset and long-term thinking. Templeton was known for his habit of investing in markets that were unpopular at the time. He famously bought 100 shares of each of the 104 companies on the New York Stock Exchange that were trading for less than $1 per share during the depths of the Great Depression. Over time, this bold move paid off handsomely, and Templeton became a billionaire. His journey underscores the importance of patience, diversification, and a contrarian approach to investing.

However, not all success stories follow a linear path. Consider the tale of Jesse Livermore, a legendary stock trader from the early 20th century. Livermore's story is one of extreme highs and lows, marked by his incredible ability to profit from market trends but also marred by substantial losses due to overconfidence and impulsive decision-making. Livermore's life underscores the importance of risk management, emotional discipline, and the dangers of letting success breed complacency.

Common Pitfalls to Avoid

While success stories inspire, they also serve as cautionary tales, highlighting the pitfalls that investors should be mindful of:

Pitfall 1: Short-Term Thinking

One of the most prevalent pitfalls is succumbing to the allure of short-term gains. Many investors, driven by the desire for quick profits, often engage in speculative trading or chase after hot stocks. This approach, more often than not, leads to disappointment and financial loss.

The wisdom from successful investors like Buffett and Graham reminds us that the path to long-term success lies in patient investing. They advocate for a mindset that focuses on the intrinsic value of assets and the potential for sustainable growth over time.

Pitfall 2: Overconfidence

Overconfidence can be a silent killer of investment portfolios. It's the belief that one's judgment is infallible and that success is guaranteed. History has shown us that even the most accomplished investors can make mistakes.

Buffett and Graham's stories teach us the importance of humility in investing. They readily admit that they do not have all the answers and that there will be instances when they are wrong. Acknowledging the limits of one's knowledge is a crucial step in avoiding overconfidence.

Pitfall 3: Emotional Decision-Making

Emotions often cloud judgment and lead to impulsive investment decisions. Fear and greed, in particular, can be powerful motivators that drive investors to make irrational choices.

Successful investors emphasize the need for emotional discipline. They have developed the ability to remain calm during market turbulence and to stick to their investment strategies even when emotions run high. This discipline is often the key factor that sets them apart from the crowd.

Continuous Learning and Growth

Investing is not a static field; it's constantly evolving. The wisdom from successful investors underscores the importance of continuous learning and adaptation.

Learning from Mistakes

Buffett once famously said, "You only have to do a very few things right in your life, so long as you don't do too many things wrong." This quote encapsulates the idea that mistakes are inevitable, but learning from them is crucial. Successful investors reflect on their missteps and use them as opportunities for growth.

Staying Informed

The world of finance is dynamic, with new technologies, economic trends, and market conditions constantly emerging. Successful investors remain avid learners, staying informed about the latest developments that may impact their investments. They read voraciously, attend conferences, and engage with experts in the field.

Adapting to Change

Perhaps the most significant lesson from successful investors is their ability to adapt. The investment landscape is never static, and the strategies that worked in the past may not necessarily work in the future. Adaptability is the key to staying ahead of the curve and navigating the ever-changing terrain of financial markets.

In today's digital age, the importance of continuous learning is more pronounced than ever. The accessibility of information and data has empowered investors to conduct in-depth research and analysis. Successful investors harness the power of technology and data analytics to make informed decisions and adapt to changing market dynamics.

Moreover, the concept of risk is ever-evolving, and successful investors recognize the need to adapt their risk management strategies accordingly. In the wake of the 2008 financial crisis, risk management practices underwent a profound transformation. Investors began placing greater emphasis on stress testing, scenario analysis, and the assessment of systemic risks. This shift underscores the importance of staying attuned to changing market dynamics and continuously refining one's risk management toolkit.

The wisdom from successful investors serves as a example for anyone seeking to thrive in the world of investing. Their stories of triumph and adversity, coupled with the cautionary tales of common pitfalls, offer invaluable insights. Moreover, their unwavering commitment to continuous learning and growth underscores the dynamic nature of investing. As we embark on our own investment journeys, let us remember that success is not a destination but a continuous pursuit of knowledge, discipline, and resilience.

Conclusion

In this journey through the world of investing, we've embarked on a quest to understand and apply the timeless wisdom of one of the greatest investors of all time, Warren Buffett. We've explored the principles that underpin his remarkable success: the power of value investing, the strategic use of options, and the cultivation of a long-term perspective. Now, as we reach the conclusion of our journey, it's time to distill these insights into a coherent and actionable investment philosophy.

The Core Principles of Buffett's Wisdom

At the heart of Warren Buffett's investment philosophy lies the core principle of value investing. It's the notion that in the cacophony of daily market fluctuations and the ceaseless stream of financial news, there are undervalued gems waiting to be discovered. Buffett's approach is not about chasing the latest trends or succumbing to the allure of speculative bets; it's about diligently seeking out companies with solid fundamentals that are trading at prices below their intrinsic value.

Value investing is not a mere strategy; it's a mindset that demands patience, discipline, and the courage to swim against the tide when necessary. It's about seeing opportunities where others see only risks, and it's about making investments that stand the test of time.

One of the pillars of Warren Buffett's success is his adept use of options, particularly index options. While options are often associated with risk, Buffett has shown us that they can be powerful tools for enhancing returns and managing risk when used judiciously. By incorporating options into his investment toolkit, Buffett has not only amplified his returns but also shielded his portfolio from adverse market movements.

The Roadmap to Success: Your Investment Plan

Now, armed with these insights, it's time to chart your course toward investment success. The first step is to craft a clear and well-defined investment plan. Your plan should reflect your financial objectives, risk tolerance, and time horizon. It should serve as your North Star, guiding your investment decisions through both calm waters and stormy seas.

In designing your portfolio, consider the lessons we've learned from Warren Buffett. Diversify your holdings across asset classes and industries, and balance risk and return to align with your goals. Remember that your portfolio is not a static entity; it requires periodic rebalancing to stay in line with your intended asset allocation.

Embrace the principles of modern portfolio theory (MPT) as you construct your portfolio. MPT reminds us that diversification can enhance returns while reducing risk. It's the tool that helps you avoid putting all your eggs in one basket, spreading your investments across a range of assets to achieve a balance that suits your risk appetite.

The Long-Term Perspective: Your Ultimate Advantage

As we've seen throughout our journey, the long-term perspective is the bedrock of successful investing. Warren Buffett's remarkable wealth is a testament to the power of compounding and the rewards of steadfastly holding quality investments over time. Your ability to harness this same power is your ultimate advantage in the world of investing.

But remember that the road to long-term success is not without its challenges. It requires emotional discipline, the ability to weather market volatility without flinching, and the courage to stay the course when others panic. The lessons of Jesse Livermore's roller-coaster career remind us that overconfidence and impulsive decision-making can lead to financial ruin. To succeed, you must remain vigilant against these pitfalls.

The Pursuit of Wisdom: A Lifelong Journey

In closing, it's essential to recognize that the pursuit of wisdom in investing is a lifelong journey. The financial landscape is ever-changing, and successful investors adapt and evolve with it. The story of Benjamin Graham, the mentor of Warren Buffett, illustrates the importance of continuous learning and refinement of one's investment approach.

In the digital age, information is at your fingertips, and the tools available for research and analysis are more powerful than ever. Embrace these resources, but do so with a discerning eye. Not all information is created equal, and the ability to separate signal from noise is a valuable skill in itself.

As you embark on your own investment journey, remember that the principles we've explored here are not just abstract concepts; they are the building blocks of financial prosperity. They are the wisdom passed down by the most successful investors of our time.

So, take a moment to reflect on the journey we've taken together—the insights, the stories, and the principles that underpin the investing prowess of Warren Buffett. Armed with this knowledge, you are now equipped to navigate the world of investing with confidence and purpose.

In the end, investing is not just about amassing wealth; it's about achieving financial security, realizing your dreams, and securing your future. Warren Buffett's enduring success is a testament to the enduring principles of value, patience, and discipline. Now, it's your turn to put these principles into action and embark on your own journey toward financial success.

As you navigate the markets, remember that investing is not a solitary endeavor. Seek the counsel of trusted advisors, stay true to your investment plan, and maintain a

long-term perspective. With diligence, determination, and
the wisdom we've uncovered together, you can indeed win
like Buffett and secure a brighter financial future.